CAUGHT IN A RIP

A personal history of
Mandurah Surf Life Saving Club

W Webb

Copyright © 2017 All rights reserved.

The moral right of Warwick Webb to be identified as the author has been asserted by him in accordance with the Copyright, Designs and Patents Act 1988. All rights reserved. No part of this book may be transmitted or used or reproduced, stored in a retrieval system, or transmitted in any form, or by any means electronic, mechanical, recording, photocopying, or in any manner whatsoever without permission in writing from the author, except for the inclusion of brief quotations in a review.

The views and opinions expressed in this work are solely those of the author. Some names have been changed to protect privacy however they reflect real people and events.

National Library of Australia Cataloguing-in-Publication entry

Creator: Webb, Warwick, author.
Title: Caught in a rip / Warwick Webb.
ISBN: 9780995432901 (paperback)
    9780995432918 (ebook)
Subjects: Webb, Warwick.
Lifesaving stations: Western Australia--Mandurah.
Surf lifesaving (Aquatic sports): Western Australia--Mandurah.
Lifesaving--Societies and clubs: Western Australia--Mandurah.

Printing: Lightning Source (USA, UK, AUS, EUR)
Interior Layout: Pickawoowoo Publishing Group
Consulting Editor: Ed Jaggard

Contents

1. Preface vii
2. Acknowledgements xi
3. The Early Days 1
4. Back From Recess 13
5. Building Site Approval 19
   Issues with Residents 23
6. A Time For Reflection 35
   Issues with Surf Life Saving 38
7. Riding on a Wave 45
8. Worried About The Future 59
9. Surf Life Saving 69
10. Dream Becomes Reality 87
    Issues with the Council 91
    Sea Wall Construction 94
    Building Construction 97
11. Fathom That 113
12. Conclusion 119

Lists

Photographs

Photograph of Mandurah Town Beach 2

Photograph from David Templeman MLA 17

Old Yacht Club, Halls Head 37

W & G Webb, B & K Bamford and M White 48

Club Members a beach clean-up October 2008 50

Club shed in Eros Reserve 52

Club life savers April 2010 71

Fourth Groyne 74

Various Nipper and competition photos 79

Seawall construction March 2012 95

Various facility construction photos 99

Brushwood laid on dunes after seawall construction 103

Official opening 14 June 2013 105

Completed club premises photographs 120

News Articles, Correspondence and Pamphlets

Mandurah Mail Article "Surf Club Site Options Floated"
9 September 2004 20

Email from Council, Subject "Eros Reserve 2007 22

Letterbox pamphlet "San Remo Sham" 2005 29

Letterbox pamphlet "Update on San Remo Park Proposal" 2005 30

Letterbox pamphlet "San Remo Park Proposal Puzzle" 2005 31

Letterbox pamphlet "Community Update San Remo Progress Association" 2006 32

Coastal Times Article "Mandurah on crest of a wave" 31 May 2006 46

Mandurah Mail Article "Surf club worried about the future" 14 August 2008 60

Coastal Times Article "Mayor Paddi Creevey" 23 September 2009 ... 66

Mandurah Mail Article Mayor Paddi Creevey 24 September 2009.... 67

Mandurah Mail Article "Planning approval granted for local surf lifesaving club" 5 January 2012 90

Southern Telegraph "New surf clubhouse under way" 23 March 2013... 98

Timeline, Map, Tables and Plans

Timeline for the club from 1996 until opening of the facility in 2013... 7

Map of the Mandurah Region 8

Table of life saving statistics 70

List of volunteer life saving services to the community 76

Building Plan 89

Table of club committee positions held.. 108

Table of Australian council numbers since 1910 114

Preface

This book is a personal account of a decade spent developing a surf life saving club in Mandurah Western Australia. A few volunteers overcame the odds when dealing with the local council and the organisation's state body who together held the power and influence in decision making. The writer joined Mandurah Surf Life Saving Club in 2003; information prior to this was gained from records and through people who were involved with the club before then.

Over 310 surf life saving facilities exist around the Australian coastline and Mandurah, a medium size West Australian town with a vast coastline just south of Perth, was without a surf life saving club until 1996. Development of a home for the club was an unnecessarily long journey that was described by some as a process that required volunteers to "wage a war" with those in power for common sense to prevail. The local council prolonged and complicated the road, leading the club to believe they were doing their best year after year with promises that they would complete a building five years before they eventually did. The council did then unashamedly ask club volunteers for greater beach services before the building was finished.

During the process there was a breakaway group from the club that set up another local club, the Port Bouvard Surf Life Saving Club, and their actions often by over enthusiastic members would make the journey even more difficult. This new group would become the main club in the area ahead of Mandurah after a very short development process. Having contacts and pushing your position vehemently can influence decision makers.

Many people, including the bureaucrats that were involved in the development process, were unaware how difficult the process was as they only dealt with or saw portions of the entire development. Some who came along during the process had little grasp of surf life saving and some chose to ignore it. This compelled the writer to document the events as a record of the tortuous development of surf life saving in Mandurah, for the club. Its purpose is also to enlighten authorities so that they may hopefully develop easier ways for volunteers to create great facilities that ultimately build more liveable communities and encourage volunteerism. If authorities do not wish for such facilities then they should be honest and say so. Or if they do they should find an alternate easier way, if it exists, for volunteers who are largely unfamiliar with all the workings of development and government.

Warwick Webb grew up on the east coast of South Africa and spent much of his early life on the beach, in large surf and developed a passion for ocean life. His family immigrated to Western Australia when he was fifteen years of age, and they recall his reluctance to leave the African coastal life. They did consider leaving him on the family farm after he spent a year at boarding school in South Africa while his family established in Australia. Half his family started moving back to South Africa within five years of immigrating to Western Australia. Warwick stayed in Australia and put himself through university in Perth, making friends with a Perth surf life saver at university who invited him to train on the Swan River and on Perth beaches. Warwick recalls a great appetite for social events and friendship amongst these surf life savers that was a magnet, so his interest in surf life saving began.

Warwick began a career in the property industry in 1988, a career that would lead him to own a business that he would later relocate to Mandurah to live a coastal life similar to the one that he was familiar with in Africa. After tragically losing his younger brother in South Africa in 1999 Warwick re-evaluated life and began seeking further interests outside working life. "My wife Georgina and I stumbled across a struggling surf life saving club near a home we had recently purchased in San Remo, Mandurah in 2003 and so the story began."

Acknowledgements

To my wife Georgina and my children, Jake and Teá, thank you for being a part of this journey. The Mandurah Surf Life Saving Club lived in our home and garage for almost ten years. Georgina and I spent eight years together on the club management committee, a decade as surf life savers and Georgina was the only club trainer for many years. Jake and Teá participated from the young age of six and five respectively. They helped on and off the beach, became knowledgeable and valued surf life savers and often provided guidance to young and old members of our club and the public. Our family of four covered most surf life saving roles and could provide a small beach patrol covering all classes of surf life savers including trainers, assessors and surf life saving support operation team members. We did have fun along the way but on occasions things became difficult and stressful, straining relationships at times. I could have spent many more hours with my family rather than following this cause. Had I been fully aware of what was ahead when we embarked on the journey I probably would not have travelled down the road, but once in it is difficult to step out. I calculate that I spent over 5000 hours of my time towards this cause and Georgina, Jake and Teá also contributed many thousands of hours of their time helping me, the club and the organisation.

It was often a thankless journey but once commenced it was too hard to give up knowing the many volunteer hours that we had invested and not wanting them to be in vain. What we endured to create this facility will hopefully leave a legacy that should see us through thick and thin in our lives ahead.

Wally Fry and Mike Smith, past presidents of Surf Life Saving WA, both supported me, my family and the club during the journey whenever we asked for help. Wally and his wife Glenis and Mike attended our club and showed a genuine interest in our development. Thank you.

Mercedes Barrie, club Life Member held the position of administrator and treasurer for many years. Thank you for your help and dedication. Ian Daniels spent four years on the committee and in particular took over club house development from me. He provided guidance and help with respect to dealing with local government.

To my friends who helped me as sounding boards for the contents of this book, in particular Mark Dove who helped me in the early days.

Thank you to all the people and club members who have helped over the years and whose company has been an inspiration to me. There are many great people in surf life saving who do amazing things. Thank you to my wife Georgina for stoically staying with me through this journey, my daughter Teá for your amiable participation and helping me create the book cover and Jennie Tanti for completing the design. My son Jake for being at my side, always willing to help and encourage me and at the age of seventeen taking on the club vice president's role.

Chapter 1

The Early Days

Mandurah is a coastal town 70 kilometres south of Perth, Western Australia. The broader region is known as the Peel Region with 50 kilometres of picturesque coastline, varying beach conditions and an estuary with interesting waterways. Mandurah has been one of Australia's fastest growth areas with a population of 80,683 in June 2013 (Source City's Profile, Mandurah Council).

During the mid 1990's the Peel Development Commission, a body that was established by the State Government to promote development in the Region, sent a letter to Surf Life Saving Western Australia querying why there was not a surf life saving club in Mandurah. Surf Life Saving Western Australia responded by sending its Vice President, Wally Fry, and its Development Officer, Jane Scott, for a series of public meetings in Mandurah. A steering group was subsequently established for the development of a surf life saving club in Mandurah. Drew Bathgate, a local, volunteered as the Chairperson of the steering committee with help from his wife Maureen.

Peel Surf Life Saving club was formed in Mandurah in 1996 when the town had a population of 37,815 people. The club located its self at Doddi's Beach in Halls Head. The club Certificate of

Incorporation shows that the club was incorporated as Peel Surf Life Saving Club on the 31st of December 1996 and the club name was changed to Mandurah Surf Life Saving Club in 2000. In 1996 the nearest surf life saving clubs to the north were Secret Harbour and Fremantle. To the south was Bunbury. Today (2016) there are three more surf life saving clubs in this region with a total of 30 clubs in Western Australia. The oldest surf life saving club in Western Australia is Cottesloe founded in 1909; the youngest two clubs are Smiths Beach, Yallingup founded in 2011 and Port Walcott, Dampier, 2015. When Peel Surf Life Saving Club formed it was the twentieth club in Western Australia.

Doddi's Beach is a popular north facing beach located on Comet Bay near the mouth of the Peel Estuary. The beach is generally characterised as a calm bay with a surf break at Robert Point and a long surf break to the north of the estuary mouth along a sand bar that eventually finishes at Town Beach. Surf skis and surf boats can ride up to 700 metres when conditions allow and the swell is a reasonable size.

Town Beach Mandurah

Comet Bay and the coast of Mandurah are sheltered by a series of offshore reefs that create safe conditions during calm seas, however

The Early Days

when the swell and tide rise these conditions can change rapidly making beaches risky and creating interesting surf for those who enjoy the ocean.

In the early days the Peel club operated a patrol at Doddi's Beach and undertook nipper activities and training while establishing itself and growing. Membership in the first season, 1996/97, grew to 52. Membership increased to 187 the following year and then 200 during the 1998/99 season. Some of the pioneers of the club were Drew Bathgate the inaugural Club President with help from his wife Maureen, together with Wally Fry and Jane Scott from Surf Life Saving WA. Tony and Julie Snelling from Bunbury SLSC assisted, developing initial club plans together with training and assessing live savers. Tony and Drew worked for the same organisation and there were discussions at work about development of surf life saving in Mandurah. Later other people including Mike Letharis, Alan White, the late Ric Roberts, the late Bob Wintle and Glenn Body among others became members of note.

A request was received by council from the club for the development of permanent facilities at Halls Head Beach during the 1997/98 season. It was envisaged that with the development of the proposed Mandurah Ocean Marina on the northern side of the Peel Estuary mouth that the Mandurah Yacht Club would relocate to the new marina site leaving their Yacht Club building in Halls Head to revert back to a community owned facility for use by groups such as the surf life saving club. Plans for the Marina had not been finalised at this stage and the option of an interim joint use arrangement being formed with the Mandurah Yacht Club by developing storage adjacent to the existing building within the Yacht Club lease area were explored. The Yacht Club premises was on council controlled land with the building being leased back to the club. As the Mandurah Ocean Marina development was not finalised and still under negotiation, the Yacht Club did not wish to commit to a joint use arrangement then as their own future was uncertain. During 2000 the Yacht Club amalgamated with the Offshore Fishing club and moved into a new building in the Marina.

Council subsequently approved the location of two club owned sea containers at Halls Head Beach in 1998 to assist with the surf live saving club's immediate storage problems for equipment. The local triathlon club shared storage with the surf life saving club and the triathlon club still had a container at this location in 2010 for storage. The surf life saving club and council continued work to find a permanent facility for the club.

Councils often referred to as local government have two components, elected councillors and paid staff. Councillors are elected by rate payers who are residents of the area. Councillors have a leader being the mayor or president, they meet frequently in a committee structure to make decisions on running the council to meet community needs and expectations. Paid staff perform all the daily functions and should implement decisions made by councillors.

During 1999, at the club's request to develop permanent facilities at Halls Head Beach, a preliminary report was written to council suggesting that council request from the Department of Land Administration, a portion of land adjacent to the Yacht Club in the City of Mandurah for the development of a storage facility for the surf life saving club. Peel SLSC contracted a design architect to provide a preliminary plan and design for a storage facility and a cost estimate. An estimated cost of $75,000 was provided for the facility for the surf life saving club that also incorporated an area for the triathlon club with toilets and showers. A request was made at the same time to council for a contribution of $50,000 from them towards the project. During this process council granted permission for a third club owned sea container at Halls Head beach, to assist with interim storage.

The Early Days

Later in 1999 the club submitted a new request to relocate to Pyramids Beach, Dawesville prior to the Halls Head storage facility proposal reaching council for approval. Council then focused their attention on the new request for the club to relocate, and they did not consider the Halls Head application. Positives and negatives were considered by council and the club for the surf life saving club to relocate to three different areas, these being Pyramids Beach, Dawesville; Fourth Groyne, Silver Sands and Eros Place, San Remo.

Pyramids Beach provided a good location for club facilities and was a popular surf beach for the public and board riders, although it was located away from the main Mandurah area. It is located in a developing estate 12 kilometres south of Mandurah town centre. Negatives were firstly limited public access, secondly the area was at the entrance to a man made channel connecting the ocean to the estuary, and sand dredging made it dangerous for the public. Pyramids Beach became unfeasible due to sand dredging being undertaken, so the other two proposed sites were evaluated.

Fourth Groyne located at Wade Street, Silver Sands had an old Bali Hut Restaurant nearby that was considered as a potential club home. However, the site was considered to be on a fragile coastline, with limited beach access and parking, no land was available for future development and there were residences very close with the potential for high resident impact. Therefore the Fourth Groyne site was not supported. Fourth Groyne does however have a great wave in a sheltered area and it is a suitable location for board riding and water skill training.

Eros Reserve, Eros Place, San Remo had a grassed park and barbecue area with parking and ablutions. However, council did not consider it as a good club location then due to the fragile coastline, poor beach access and resident impact. It was later recognised that there were no easy answers to the club's request for a facility and council believed that sites would be available in the future through pending developments at Dawesville, Halls Head and the proposed Marina. Council recommended that the club stay in Halls Head for the 1999/2000 season and they also suggested that a strategic plan was needed for the club to ensure that its organisational structure was in place with adequate resources available to deal with these difficult variables. Council did not initiate this strategic plan. It is felt they should have assisted in the development of this plan, with help from surf life saving's state body. The council had a large interest in planning of the rapidly growing town and beach safety considerations should have been their responsibility due to potential liability for accidents on beaches in their jurisdiction. Surf life saving club buildings are normally located on council land and buildings are owned by the council.

When volunteer organisations locate in areas, approvals are required from local government and state bodies. These bodies should map out clear development pathways early for volunteer organisations so that direction, responsibilities and tasks are understood. This together with guidance and assistance will build relationships through understanding and trust. This did not happen.

The club would be left in limbo for many years without this strategic plan and this would contribute to a later split in the club when different club people wished to be in different locations, due to a lack of planning and vision on the part of the council. A brief timeline for the club from 1996 until the club facility was built in 2013 is below.

The Early Days

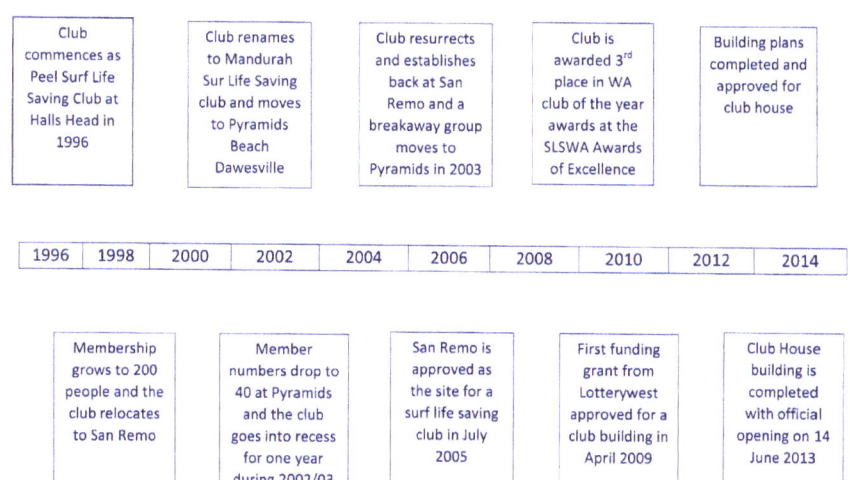

Timeline

An early surf life saving report; "Local Surf Risk and Management Ratings developed by Surf Life Saving WA" for various beach locations in Mandurah with ratings of 1 to 10, 10 being very risky, ranked Pyramids Beach and San Remo as "8" with Fourth Groyne near San Remo also being an "8". All other Mandurah Beaches were rated below this rating with Doddi's Beach being the safest. San Remo suffers a dumping beach swell that can cause injury when conditions are bad. Broken bones or spinal injuries are a risk. Pyramids Beach has a surf break and dangerous rips and currents can develop. The report stated "Risk at these beach locations in the City of Mandurah will increase as access and attendance increases at these locations."

Club membership grew to around 200 soon after commencement and later in 1999 the expanding club relocated to San Remo to accommodate a maturing development whilst also seeking a beach with waves. During 2000 under a new management committee Peel Surf Life Saving Club renamed itself Mandurah Surf Life Saving Club and relocated to Pyramids Beach at Dawesville. Pyramids Beach as mentioned earlier is a surf beach located to the south of the man made Dawesville Cut Channel that links Peel Estuary to the ocean. The channel was built in the early 1990's to allow greater water flow into the estuary and thus improve water quality in the estuary that was affected by runoff from farming activities upstream.

Map of the Mandurah area is depicted below.

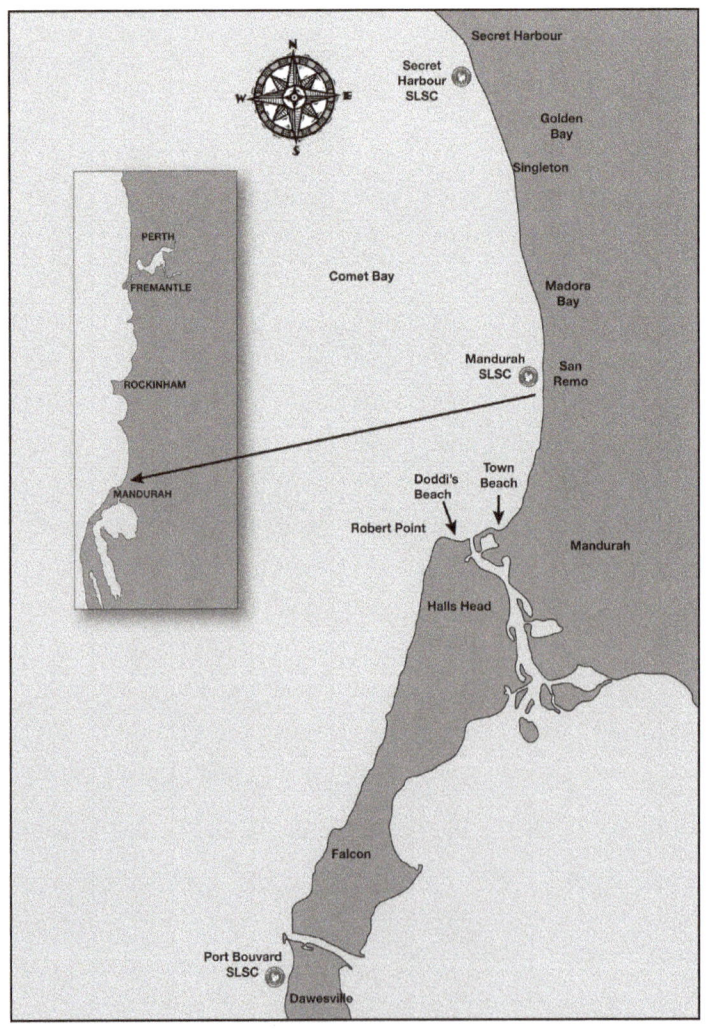

Map of Mandurah Coastline (scale 1:130 000)

In 2000/01 season after the move to Pyramids Beach membership dropped and the following season member numbers dropped again to 40. Mandurah Surf Life Saving Club then went in to recession for a season during 2002/03. When the club went into recession industry standards then stated that club equipment would be provided to the neighbouring surf life saving clubs on a loan basis, the state body would hold a register of the equipment and that equipment would be returned to the original club when activities resumed. The club maintained its bank account and its administration records during the recession period. The neighbouring clubs of Binningup and Secret Harbour gained some of the equipment with the balance being held by a number of Mandurah club members. The state body did not maintain a register and it would take some time to regain the equipment when the club resumed.

The club had been in discussion with Mandurah council since inception regarding establishing a club house and base. Past club members recall a long fruitless, frustrating time trying to establish a base. Subsequent members would also encounter this and would almost need to wage an unnecessary, time consuming war against authorities and other bodies to establish clubrooms. Club operation and planning for any organisation is difficult when the future is in limbo for prolonged periods.

Surf life saving clubs across the country generally establish a mutually beneficial relationship with their local council that allows their existence while they provide a safer environment for council controlled beaches in return. There is legal precedent to show that liability for beach accidents can be costly for councils.

The Mandurah council had provided the club with a small annual contribution of $2,000 in return for life saving services up until 2002. This contribution commenced in 1997 at $1,000 per annum and funds were used for life saving and training equipment purchases and operation costs. The club raised funds via memberships, grants and any other means to provide its life saving services. A club treasurer's report dated 19 August 1997 shows the club had $883.50 in the bank.

When the club returned from recession in 2003 the council did not reinstate their contribution, despite many requests. Later, in a letter dated 13 April 2006 it formally declined to do so. In the letter that council sent to the club they stated amongst other things that "Increasing levels of visitors safety and minimisation of risk within the City's beach and coastal environments have been a significant focus of council"…"The City of Mandurah has been a major supporter of the MSLSC in the endeavour to secure new facilities at Eros Reserve, San Remo. As the City will be providing significant monetary funds towards the completion of this project, Council feel it is meeting its obligation towards the MSLSC and the community and will unfortunately be unable to provide a yearly donation." Their significant monetary contribution towards the building eventuated in 2013 after the club raised more than half the funds for the facility cost. MSLSC in surf life saving circles refers to a club at Mullaloo and Mandurah is MHSLSC. Council rarely got this correct despite many notifications.

The annual funding contribution was only discussed again by council when they requested more services from the club in 2012. The club was happy to oblige, but requested some funding as all club services are self funded requiring expensive equipment and most councils in the state were now contributing by an annual service fee. Mandurah council seemed to acknowledge in 2012 that a contribution was warranted but said it would take, a year or two to implement the funding. This funding eventuated in 2015.

A surf life saving club's primary role is to keep beaches safe, sport and competition are secondary, being a way to keep volunteer surf life savers fit and also a way to support member retention. A surf life saver is required to undertake a minimum of sixteen hours of patrol service before he or she is eligible to compete at surf life saving sports events. Many clubs in WA are paid in some form for their volunteer life saving services by councils as clubs are self funded and require a reasonable turnover to support operations. Some councils will pay a service fee then charge the club a smaller amount for rent or a maintenance levy for their club rooms. Very few clubs in WA own their own facilities and most rent them from local councils. Surf Life Saving WA manages a paid lifeguard service usually paid for by councils with life guards coming from clubs. Mandurah council chose not to acknowledge the role of a surf life saving club for many years, preferring to categorise our surf life saving club as a sports club so as to avoid a service charge, despite many attempts to explain this. There are no sports clubs that I am aware of that provide a similar level of community service or beach safety as their primary purpose. A volunteer fire brigade may have similarities.

Chapter 2

Back From Recess

Mandurah Surf Life Saving Club was resurrected and reformed in 2003 at Town Beach in Mandurah by members of the original administration group after a year in recession. Unfortunately when the club went into recession the disruption meant that some members left surf life saving and others moved permanently to Secret Harbour club which is an established club 14 kilometres to the north of Mandurah Town Centre. Membership grew slowly as the club re-birthed in 2003 and the club relocated to San Remo again. A breakaway group started as Port Bouvard Surf Life Saving Club in December 2003. Port Bouvard was the 27th club of WA when it formed. The founding president of Port Bouvard was Alan White with the late Ric Roberts as the Vice President. Both Alan and Ric are past members of a large Perth surf life saving club. Ric passed away just before their club house was completed in early 2010 from an illness. He gave his heart and soul and worked daily for many years towards the development of their club and its building.

After a year long recess during 2002/03, Mandurah again, under the leadership of President Drew Bathgate along with support from

Wally Fry, Rick Fry as Club Captain, Joan Fry as Secretary with Debbie Boekelman taking care of juniors, set about re-establishing the club at San Remo in 2003. My wife Georgina, our children Jake and Teá and I became involved in the club shortly after relocating our business to Mandurah from Perth, when we purchased a home in San Remo in mid 2003.

The club held its open day in Eros Reserve, San Remo one Sunday morning. Georgina and I agreed that it would be in our interests to join as we planned to live permanently in the area. It was also in our best interests to be involved with the development of a club that was in close proximity to our home. The club was small with membership just under 40 and an enthusiastic management committee. I was familiar with the ocean, enjoyed beach activities and was broadly familiar with surf life saving as I had socialised at City of Perth Surf Life Saving Club when at university.

Within a short time Georgina and I were both on the committee and we had provided storage at our home for club equipment. I became vice president and Georgina was appointed as secretary treasurer. During 2004 the club restructured and Wally Fry a past president of Surf Life Saving WA (SLSWA) became president of the club. Wally was living north of Perth and he attended the club when available. Mike Gray assumed the role of Club Captain with Marlene Renton, Mercedes Barrie and Paul Timms as committee members. Equipment was basic and turnover was about $2000 per annum during our first season.

Binningup and Secret Harbour clubs were helpful and returned our equipment that was loaned to them when the club went into recession. The main surf boat that belonged to Mandurah Surf Life Saving Club was with a senior member of the new Port Bouvard Surf Life Saving Club. This person was previously with Mandurah Surf Life Saving Club from 1999 to 2001 when he resigned from the club. He had no club membership or access rights to hold the boat however he had possession and would not return the boat to Mandurah SLSC. The surf boat was purchased by Mandurah SLSC from Swanbourne SLSC and Mandurah had documents to show this together with receipts for full payment. There was no outstanding money owed for the boat. Sponsorship rights to the boat had also been sold. Possession and ownership of the boat became a protracted issue that was reported to Surf Life Saving WA and Surf Life Saving Australia. Both organisations were unable to resolve the issue and eventually this was reported to the Police. The president of Port Bouvard Surf Life Saving Club subsequently stood down over this messy issue. The Port Bouvard Surf Sports & Life Saving Club (as it was then known), Annual Report States "President ... (Resigned June 2004) Ric Roberts Appointed President 1st July 2004". At the same time the treasurer also resigned and Ric Roberts assumed that role as well.

Correspondence dated November 2004 from the grievance officer of Surf Life Saving Australia states; "a. That both Parties acknowledge that the organisational Grievance mediation process run its course, with the parties still in dispute. b. Given the nature of the Grievance, both parties seek legal counsel in order to effect a legally binding resolution to the issues raised."

A With-out Prejudice letter from Port Bouvard Surf Sports & Life Saving Club dated 29 April 2004 claimed that Port Bouvard Club would not return the boat as $2,700 was owing to one of their members and he was exercising a lien. This lien was not substantiated, nor was it produced. Neither the lien nor any other boat issues were raised or recorded when these members resigned from the Mandurah club years earlier to move to set up another club at Port Bouvard. Sponsorship monies paid for the boat were not accounted for but may have been spent on the boat. The boat had Mandurah SLSC painted in various places on the hull and trailer.

During 2004 a member of Mandurah SLSC went to retrieve the boat from a member of Port Bouvard Surf Sports & Life Saving Club, after discussions between the parties and SLSA to resolve the issue with resolution appearing imminent; however the person holding the boat said he was feeling unwell on arrival. The Mandurah representative left and the boat was not collected. The boat was then moved from that location to an unknown location and a letter was sent to Mandurah SLSC from Port Bouvard SLSC stating that Mandurah had caused their member distress by trying to retrieve the boat. Resolution of this dispute took many hours of my time and eventually after about 18 months of messy discussions and finally a lengthy meeting we resolved the issue and the boat was returned to Mandurah SLSC. This was an unfortunate event that had damaged the image of both clubs and surf life saving in the area. This event resulted in strained relations between the clubs that festered for many years.

During the 2004 season we would trailer our equipment from various homes to Eros Reserve car park in San Remo for club activities and then carry equipment down to the beach manually. This manual handling which involved a stairway was hard work for the few that did it. We would arrive an hour or two before patrols and stay an hour or two after patrols to pack up.

Later one of our members Matthew Dundas provided an old four wheel drive vehicle to the club and we gained access a kilometre down the beach and towed all the equipment up to San Remo. This helped, but was not without its own problems as access was not good and we regularly got bogged. We needed better access and a good vehicle.

Mandurah Surf Lifesaving Club
Sunday 28th November 2004

Photograph from David Templeman MLA

The club grew during 2004 and re-established itself as a probationary club of Surf Life Saving WA. The club was affiliated prior to going into recession however returned as a probationary club. The surf life saving system has affiliated clubs that are clubs who meet all the life saving criteria to operate beach patrols and carry greater status versus probationary clubs in the organisation. Probationary clubs are generally the newer clubs working to build up capacity and experience for affiliation. Probationary clubs do not get a vote at SLSWA, are not eligible to compete in sports events, do not pay affiliation fees and are not eligible for all life saving grants.

Chapter 3

Building Site Approval

We approached the council again in 2003 when returning from recession, and re-established dialogue for gaining clubrooms. We received mixed responses in early meetings with the council regarding clubrooms. The council agreed to conduct a survey in conjunction with Surf Life Saving WA and other professionals to establish a beach location within city precincts for our club. During the survey the group considered Town Beach, but agreed that the area had been planned and was already partly developed without an area set aside for a life saving facility contrary to what they had said years earlier. Some council officers also stated that the land was too expensive for a surf life saving club. Henson Street, Silver Sands was also considered but did not have enough land to build club rooms. Madora was too far out of town and San Remo provided the best fit at that time. All parties including Surf Life Saving WA agreed that from San Remo the club could develop into a mobile club that would move between Halls Head and Madora via water craft and vehicles, with the possibility of outpost patrols in the future.

Eventually after an exhaustive survey and community consultation process Eros Reserve, San Remo was approved by council in July 2005 as the site for a surf life saving club building. I had attended many meetings with various council staff and consultants in 2004/05 during the survey. Mike Smith the President of Surf Life Saving WA at that time, assisted me greatly and attended meetings as requested. Mike was heckled by locals on a number of occasions and in particular after a council meeting in 2005 when San Remo was approved as the site for a surf life saving facility. There was a small group of locals who did not support the club being built at San Remo.

Surf club site options floated

EROS Place Reserve in San Remo and Henson Street, Mandurah have been proposed as potential sites for the Mandurah Surf Lifesaving Club.

This follows in principle support from the City's Planning, Community Development and Sustainability Committee meeting last week.

Council officers will start community and stakeholder consultation on both location options.

City chief executive Mark Newman said the City had been liaising with the lifesaving club to investigate a suitable location for the new facility.

"At this stage, the City is only considering the location of the Surf Lifesaving Club, with future concept and development plans to be assessed in accordance with planning policies, environmental and other approvals," Mr Newman said.

Planning for the surf lifesaving facilities is in its infancy with funding options currently being investigated, incorporating the City's $200,000 allocation identified for 2008/9 within Mandurah's Capital Works plan.

Following approval City officers will undertake extensive community consultation to gather information for the future facility and develop a design concept for the preferred location. The recommendation will be debated at a full council meeting on December 15.

(Mandurah Mail 9 December 2004)

Building Site Approval

Eros Reserve is a medium size park located on the beach in San Remo with the land being owned by the crown. Management is vested with the Mandurah council via a management order. An enquiry with the Land Titles Offices reveals that the management order was vested with the council in 1978. An amendment to reflect council's approval in 2005 for a surf life saving facility in the reserve was required. This is a relatively simple process of amending the management order that is registered on the land title. It would be 21st November 2007 before the council completed this task after submitting a formal request to the Department of Planning and Infrastructure in April 2007, a 7 month process for the amendment. The site was approved for a surf life saving facility in July 2005 yet council delayed 21 months after this to seek the amendment. The club was continually told by the council that there were complex land tenure issues, including by the Mayor on 29 January 2007 "I can appreciate your frustration but we are certainly fully supportive of your club and appreciate all the members do. Unfortunately the land issues are so much more protracted in the case of the club." The management order when amended permitted "the development and management of a surf lifesaving club within lot 2723" and granted the council power to lease the facility "for any term not exceeding twenty one (21) years".

Councils have the ability to slow a club room development process down if they choose and in our case they would not be totally transparent about their delays, rather leading us on each year while extending and pushing the process out contrary to what they told us. In an article about our club in the *Mandurah Mail* dated 9 December 2004 council suggested that $200,000 would be identified in 2008/09 for a surf life saving project. This allocation was not properly identified and did not eventuate for our facility. These delays and the inability to stick to plans were frustrating and a process that was not conducive to building a mutually trusting relationship.

Council staff advised me a few times during 2004 that we would be in a building with an established permanent home before Port Bouvard Surf Life Saving Club. On 22 January 2007 council supplied a written timeline for construction of a facility for our club commencing in mid 2007, with opening and commencement of operations in December 2008. Then council did not support our application for funding, only ranking us as third with funding bodies when funding was only available for up to two projects. One of the officers who prepared the documents did say on one occasion that the Mandurah Surf Life Saving Club project was not their pet project. In another meeting with a council manager and his director, the director suggested that paid council staff ran the council and the wishes of elected members of the council did not matter. Elected members should bring forward the will of their constituents and paid staff should then carry these actions out contrary to what was said. I avoided this director from then on.

An email from council sent in 2007 with the club construction timeline follows:

Subject: Eros Reserve

Hi All

Just a progress report on the Mandurah Surf Life Saving Club facilities - Eros Reserve.

Since the last email and the adoption of the master plan in November 2006 we have been following through on preliminary discussions with DPI regarding land tenure. It would appear as a result of these discussions the land tenure negotiations will be simpler and quicker than first thought.

In terms of next stages, the following overall time frames are anticipated as being;

to June 2007	Finalise land tenure negotiations with DPI
April / May 2007	Advertise for architects
June 2007	Council meeting to appoint architects
July - October 2007	Design development and costing
October 2007	CSRFF Funding application
November 2007	Regional Partnerships application to DOTARS
March 2008	Outcome of funding applications
April / May 2008	Advertise Main Building contract and select builder
July 2008	Commencement of construction
December 2008	Opening and Commencement of operations

With regards to the steering group, as the master planning process has now been completed and the next few steps are internal processes there is probably no need to meet until such time as the architect is appointed and consultation occurs during the design development stage (July 07).

In the mean time, should you have any enquiries please do not hesitate to email or call our department on 9550

I had suggested to a council staff person during 2004 that I was prepared to set a day or two aside and arrange a fact finding trip up and down the coast with him to various Perth surf life saving clubs to study their buildings and operation styles. He replied that he knew enough about surf life saving and that I did not need to do this. His actions showed that he was not as fully informed as he thought about the surf life saving industry and that his style of behaviour was prevalent amongst some in the council. As an example, in all my dealings over a ten year period with council on behalf of the club regarding building a facility that council would own, on their beach, not once had a paid staff member of council requested attendance at any of our activities or club meetings to gain an understanding of our operations, yet they were always happy to tell us what they thought we needed, and struggled to listen when we suggested otherwise. I unsuccessfully invited staff to our club on a number of occasions.

I formed a building committee for our proposed club house development after San Remo was approved as the location for our club house in 2005. The committee included members from our club, members from other established clubs with surf life saving experience, a builder and a home owner in close proximity to the site. We set about developing a master plan with council for our facility. This master plan was prepared by council engaged consultants and was finalised in 2007.

Issues with Residents

The process of selecting San Remo for a surf life saving facility involved a community consultation phase that was often emotional and messy. Certain home owners arranged meetings at their homes to oppose the San Remo location. These meetings were emotionally charged and nonsensical at times. I was personally attacked on occasions and recall an unpleasant incident with things said about my family at a community meeting at the Meadow Springs Country Club by a home owner in San Remo. The next afternoon a local resident who was now in a small group that opposed the facility location knocked on my door to try and tell me what she thought the person had meant the previous night with his unpleasant comments. This attempt to justify the comments did not wash well with me as such comments could not be justified. These anti people were later provided with documents for the dormant San Remo Progress Association and set about using this as a vehicle to push their "anti surf life saving club location at San Remo" message. Luckily for us, the group was not large or well organised.

One member of this anti group undertook a letter box drop of negative pamphlets and another door knocked areas with a petition. We had many club members in the area that engaged with these people and reported activities back to me. The anti group never attracted a large following, although they professed to have good support.

A member of this group volunteered as a committee member for the steering group that developed a plan for a surf life saving building in San Remo. He promptly pushed to move the location of the proposed building from the front of his house to the front of the house of one of the other progress association members. This second person then took it out on me and rang council rangers and any other person in authority to persistently complain about any silly little thing that he could. Much to his disgust his petty complaints did not carry weight or substance or result in any findings against me. Council rangers would act on his complaints and visit me. After a number of visits I started informing the rangers that they were playing into this person's anti campaign against me by acting on all his complaints, visiting me unnecessarily which was becoming annoying as I was doing nothing wrong. Rangers repeatedly said that they had to investigate every complaint. I asked that they be a little wiser about this person, but it went on for a lengthy period before rangers eventually stopped questioning me. This was not a pleasant experience.

Around 2009 a person commenced photographing me and club members on the beach including children training in bathers on the beach. This was often done whilst he was in the sand dunes with a large camera lens or in a way that he was trying to disguise what he was doing. It went on for years despite our requests that he stop and eventually this resulted in police visiting him. On one occasion many club members the majority being under 20 years of age confronted him at the beach and explained why they did not like his actions as it was invasive on their privacy. One of our young members needed their identity protected for welfare reasons. The photographer replied that he was not aware of that and had not thought of the scenario.

The council asked me to attend various community meetings as the club president during the consultation process and during one meeting in Meadow Springs in 2004 regarding locating a surf life saving facility in San Remo a local resident who was vocal about the issue told the meeting that he was an ex surf life saver, and that he had much knowledge about surf life saving. He also suggested that we should not have the building in San Remo as he was a rat bag and drank a lot, when he was younger and that we would do the same. We were a little bemused by his comments. Later, towards the end of the meeting in question time he requested that a club delegate answer a question. I was summoned to the front of the room and he asked "how was the club going to transport rescue equipment up and down the beach as we did not have a vehicle?" When I asked what equipment he was referring to he replied "the surf rescue reel". This piece of equipment was outdated and had not been used for years. After his earlier comments it was a little too easy to reply that this piece of equipment had not been used for many years so there was no issue, much to the amusement of others. This infuriated the questioner and set a scene for a man who would demonstrate unreasonable behaviour towards me and the club for years to come.

I recall a meeting during the consultation process after a letter box drop of pamphlets headed "San Remo Sham!" About 80 people gathered on the front lawn of a large nearby ostentatious residence when the owner made a negative address from his verandah about a proposed ugly council development on the beach front and another local resident in the crowd stopped the speaker and said "turn around and look at your f__ken ugly monstrosity, it is visible from James Service Reef 5 miles out to sea." The whole meeting erupted and deteriorated from that point. An elected council member at the meeting who had been verbally challenged walked off and said "I do not need to put up with this bullsh_t." This home owner displayed a sign on his home for a lengthy period after San Remo was approved as the site for a surf life saving club in 2005. The person who asked the home owner to turn around and look at his "ugly monstrosity" later joined the club with his family, becoming a good friend of ours and a valued contributor to the club.

The owner of the residence would also complain that a surf life saving club would attract out of control 18th and 21st birthday parties that would be bad for the area. Part of my involvement as a nearby resident was to set up a club with a structure that would not allow these activities instead fostering a fun family environment. It was however not too long before this property owner had an 18th birthday for a relative at his home that went all night. At 8am the next day party goers were still in the park, car parking area and surrounding areas and the streets were covered with broken glass and debris. I spent over an hour with other residents cleaning his mess while this man just looked at us. His true colours were being shown and most people in the neighbourhood started to see that he was not really a part of our community. He did not reside in the community, nor was he a positive contributor, yet he was very quick to boldly express his views about what the community should or should not do.

Council's community consultation resulted in a collection or data base of comments that would be considered in the decision making process. These comments were provided to me in hard copy by a council person for review. I reviewed the large document containing 67 responses on the evening it was provided to me and noted 47 positive comments and 20 who did not support San Remo as the building site, but most of the 20 did support surf life saving as long as it was in another location and many suggested Madora or central Mandurah as alternate sites. Some of the positive comments were qualified and supported the proposal as long as other studies e.g. traffic, environmental and engineering advice was sought. Some comments were a little emotional and some of the negative people had multiple family members respond from one address with each response counted separately. One family did not want the club built due to environmental reasons that would disturb sand dunes yet in other correspondence were suggesting that sand dunes in front of their home should be knocked down for their benefit. The person in council who provided me with the responses called me the following day and said that he should not have provided the information to me, so I promptly returned it and did not stir the issue any further. However this document was provided to me again many years later.

There was much misinformed speculation and hysteria about what the facility would comprise, including that it was a two storey building with licensed premises and commercial uses. I was criticised about these things even before they had been planned or properly considered. One thing I did do during the process was push for a single level facility that blended into the residential area, was recessed into the dunes and could be located as close to the ocean as possible, with the possibility for a limited club alcohol license. These were all ways to try and reduce the impact of the facility on residents. Surf life saving facilities commonly locate on public land in ocean front locations such as Eros Reserve and use of this public land should not be restricted or governed by a few who live opposite it. I had even suggested to a number of these negative people that they join the steering groups and committees to have input and help build something that they could be happy with as it would be almost impossible to stop the development. Only one "anti" person joined a council group and no one accepted our offers to have input.

The following four pages are copies of letter box pamphlets that were circulated in San Remo during 2005 and 2006 in an attempt to stop the development of a surf life saving building in San Remo. Some personal information is blanked out.

SAN REMO SHAM!

At a **City of Mandurah council meeting** on December 15, 2004 (6 MONTHS AGO), discussions were held regarding a future location for a surf club.

Two proposed sites were identified: **Henson Street Reserve in Silver Sands** and **Eros Place Reserve in San Remo**. Council promised in writing that any **future development** in either of these two areas was **subject** to a favourable response through a **community agreeance and consultation process**. Council also confirmed that Eros Place Reserve was its preferred site for the surf club.

In the past week (6 MONTHS LATER), some San Remo residents have received written correspondence from the City of Mandurah regarding the proposed development of community facilities – including a surf club – at the two sites. As of Thursday, May 19, many San Remo residents still have no knowledge of the proposal nor received any correspondence from council.

The City of Mandurah's correspondence clearly doesn't disclose all the facts in relation to the development. The correspondence sent by the council has failed to fully explain the total proposal as discussed at the meeting – which includes **plans for a deli, café and community hall**, as well as the surf club. Council has also **encouraged further commercial development** at the proposed site. Why is council hiding behind a surf club, when it's really a commercial development that includes the mentioned items?

Enquiries to the City of Mandurah have resulted in dismissive and evasive responses. WHY? And why, if there were two recommended sites, has the council asked only the residents of San Remo to put their case forward? Why haven't the residents of Silver Sands been asked to do the same?

Furthermore, if these recommendations were made six months ago, why weren't residents of San Remo informed then, instead a week before (and some none at all) the council's planned community consultation meeting with residents on the matter on May 23-24?

Whilst this is not a cut-and-dry situation, we as residents still have time to preserve the tranquillity and spirit of the area we chose to live in and to stop encroachment of commercialism on San Remo.

IT HAS TO STAY THE SANCTUARY THAT IT IS TODAY!

If you are concerned and/or are not aware of the full extent of the development, please attend:

San Remo Residents Meeting
Sunday, 22 May, 10.30am
Ormsby Tce (█████████) San Remo

There are a lot of issues and questions to be raised and this is our only opportunity to prepare and present any concerns on the matter to the Monday and Tuesday night consultation meetings planned by the council at the Meadow Springs Golf Club. Our Ward Councillors have also been made aware of our Sunday meeting and their presence is anticipated. If you wish to discuss any issues in the meantime, contact ████ on ████████, ██████ or ████████.

San Remo Sham

UPDATE ON SAN REMO PARK PROPOSAL

Dear fellow residents,

A meeting was held at Mandurah Council Chambers on Tuesday 5th of July (PCDS sub committee meeting) regarding the proposed surf club and commercial development on Eros Reserve.

The outcome of that meeting was –

- Councillors deemed that Eros Reserve remained the preferred site for the surf club and future development. (2 councillors – Rodgers and Wilson voted against)
- An overwhelming majority of residents were totally opposed to the location of the proposed development and yet 2 of our 3 North Ward councillors (Les Atkins and Ron Wortley) neither presented or supported the feedback of constituents.
- The concerns of residents were mainly –
  - **No buffer zone** between the houses and the proposed club building. Some councillors expressed serious concern about the lack of buffer zone and agreed that it seemed insufficient.
  - **Traffic access** was a major concern – no traffic management studies have been undertaken and *a traffic plan will not fix the problem.*
- The possibility of **vandalism, anti-social behaviour** and disturbance at night were not considered and it was suggested by a council staff member that the closest residents would act as protectors of the development.
- The stance on **no liquor licensing** was softened.

REMEMBER THE COMMUNITY CONSULTATION MEETINGS? *Remember the promises?*
1. If the majority of residents rejected the proposal Council would relocate it. **NOT KEPT.**
2. No Liquor Licence if we didn't want it for the facility. **NOT KEPT.** Council endorses Liquor licences application for parties and will administer
3. A small storage/club facility. **NOT KEPT.** The plan shown to us missed some rooms and is now being discussed as "Stage One". What will Stage Two be?

Can we believe any future promises Council may make?

The recommendation that planning goes ahead for Eros Park will be taken to the **FULL COUNCIL** meeting on the **19th of JULY**. To ensure that all councillors are fully aware of our community views (and don't just rely on an internal report) we urge ALL residents to make their opinions heard by all council members.

There are two ways that you can ensure that your views are heard –

1. **Contact as many councillors as possible** by phone or fax and express your views! (see over for ph/fx details)

2. **Be present at the next full Council meeting on the 19th of July** (Tuesday next week) at **5pm** at Council Chambers to voice your opinion and to show your united alliance.

This meeting is the last opportunity that residents have before motions are passed sealing the future of our reserve.

Make your voice be heard – call a councillor today!

Let us show our resolve and determination to stop this development in our reserve.

Update on San Remo Park Proposal

SAN REMO PARK PROPOSAL PUZZLE

You should know that new VITAL INFORMATION is now available since the first public meeting on May 23.

- **OMISSIONS IN REPORT TO RESIDENTS**

  *The MCC Eros Park proposal as mailed to residents to fully inform them prior to the May 23 meeting omitted significant points from the report provided by Gordon McMile to Council Committee for their Nov 30 meeting.

  - Mention is made of a **double storey building** in the "McMile" report but omitted in the report to residents;
  - The fact that there should be a **12 month delay in design and planning** for beach behaviour stabilisation after groyne installation for environmental reasons was omitted;
  - The fact that site access from Fremantle Road could prove **problematic** was omitted.

- **CONCERNS RE DEVELOPMENT**
- A building design was presented to the meeting and if you went away believing that this was what would eventually be built **you are horribly mistaken.**
- At Council meeting 7 June it was discussed that $300,000 + $100,000 be allocated for **STAGE ONE (!)** of the development!
- Liquor Licence. The Council stated it is impossible to guarantee that a licence will never be granted. MSLSC members are talking about it already.
- At that meeting it was accepted that the preference of the MSLSC was San Remo. They now state that it doesn't matter where they go as long as they get a facility. SLSWA now would be happy with another location other than San Remo.
- G McMile said at the meeting that beach usage figures presented by a resident were outdated. This has since been found to be incorrect.

- **OTHER IMPORTANT POINTS**
- Since 1975 the residents of San Remo have been fighting **ANY** future development in the coastal dune system closer than 100m setback in accordance with Mandurah and WA Government Coastal Strategies.
  - This proposal has no setback in a designated endangered dune system.
  - Do you wish to see 30 years of community endeavour sacrificed?
- The future of the cycle club which has a long history of operations from the Eros Park car park has apparently been ignored completely.
- The Mandurah Coastal Management Plan 2004 – 2009 recommended 18 pertinent items - one that Eros Park be left untouched other than for environmental reasons. This appears to have been overturned by Council after personal representation by the MSLSC. **Why?**
- From comments recently made it appears that the Club has no concrete plans for future expansion. **Can this be true? Stage 2 is already under discussion in Council!**

Mandurah has already set a high standard with recent developments addressing future expansion, local community and environmental aspects............

WHY SHOULD ALL THIS BE IGNORED IN REGARD TO SAN REMO?

DON'T TAKE A RISK........

SAY NO TO _ANY_ NEW DEVELOPMENT IN THE PARK

This is to be delivered to residents prior to being asked personally to offer their opinion on the Eros Park proposal.
*GM031.doc and file ref: (A01517) (author: Gordon McMile).

Remo Park proposal puzzle

Community Update
San Remo Progress Association

For those who are unaware or new to the area, the SRPA was reformed in June 2005 after a number of years suspended due to minimal activity in the local community. The reformation was carried out as a result of a community meeting called about proposed developments on Eros Reserve, and the association has continued since that time with involvement in this development and with other community related items.

Issues discussed and actioned over the last year can be summarised as follows:

June 05	• Eros Reserve location for MSLSC and Community Facilities
July 05	• Poor state of grassed areas in San Remo, and reticulation concerns • Eros Reserve location for MSLSC and Community Facilities
Sept 05	• Road works on Ormsby Terrace • Safety concerns resultant from the beach & dune re-nourishment programme • Eros Reserve location for MSLSC and Community Facilities
Oct 05	• Missing signage at the beach (fishing, fish watch & sand boarding) • State of temporary power line repairs at feeder transformer • Earthing issue affecting local broadband users • Faulty street lighting • Eros Reserve location for MSLSC and Community Facilities
Dec 05	• Dune demolition and restoration efforts • Faulty street lighting • Eros Reserve location for MSLSC and Community Facilities
Feb 06	• Informal meeting – sole topic being SRPA Involvement in Community Consultation for MSLSC and Community Facilities
May to July 06	• Member of working group for master planning Eros Reserve (in conjunction with City of Mandurah and MSLSC)
Oct 06	• Feedback Session on Eros Reserve master planning process

The SRPA would like to call a community meeting to provide the following :
1. Feedback about the **Master Planning of Eros Reserve for the future MSLSC & Community facilities**, as this activity has been underway with SRPA, MSLSC, City of Mandurah & an Urban Designer for a number of months and is now nearing completion and submission to Council.
2. *A forum for the general community* to feedback any items they would like the association to address
3. Opportunity to **become a member** and receive invitation to meetings, a copy of minutes, and / or to become more actively involved in any activities.

The relatively short notice for the meeting is as a result of a one week timeframe to provide community feedback MCC on item 1 above, and a low attendance by the local community at the Citys' Master Plan presentation held Wednesday 4th Oct at 8pm.

When	Sunday 8th October @ 2:30pm
Where -	Eros Reserve Car park & BBQ area

San Remo Progress Association
Providing a focal point for community interests in the San Remo area.
Phone: 08 9581 9021 or 08 95817575   Fax: 08 9581 7979
Email: srra@SanRemo.net.au   Web: srra.sanremo.net.au

Community update SRPA

Building Site Approval

During 2004 and 2005 I spent many hours talking to people, lobbying, attending meetings and undertaking deputations to council in order to provide details of the benefits to the community for having a surf life saving facility in San Remo. I was a novice at doing this and recall nervous, daunting times speaking to council people. I had called all Mandurah councillors a few weeks prior to a council vote for our surf life saving facility location at San Remo and asked them if they required any further information to make their decision and if they had any unanswered questions, I would attempt to answer them. Most were happy with the proposal and I gauged about 80% support from their comments. A few days prior to the vote I called them all again and asked if they had any further questions. They all had a similar view, except one councillor who said he could not support us as a senior person from the Port Bouvard SLSC had passed disparaging comments to him about me and our club and that meant he would withdraw his vote of support. I questioned him and he said he would not elaborate. I was obviously disappointed and concerned about this behaviour.

The majority of councillors supported the vote. However, the councillor who had previously supported us did not vote in our favour at the meeting. I later challenged the person who had made these negative comments and raised this with Surf Life Saving WA as it was not great behaviour from within our organisation. There were no answers from the person who had passed these negative comments other than a cough and splutter and little reaction from senior people in the organisation.

Unfortunately when a decision is made on a public issue such as the approval of our club building there will always be people who choose not to accept the outcome and this can result in bad behaviour. An example was when a bag of bait, meat, open tins of food, pet food and offal was placed 50 metres offshore in an area that our surf life saving club trained on Sunday mornings. My wife was training club members and kids in the ocean when she called out with concern that something had caught hold of her and was pulling her under the water. I swam over rapidly and dived under to find a very heavy bag with rope around it that was caught on her legs. I then managed to free her in a reasonable time and averted something more serious. We pulled the bag ashore and were surprised with its contents. Unfortunately the story made its way to the media with photographs after I had asked people to ignore it. The news appeared in the *West Australian* and one of the main TV stations arrived on my door step the next day. I promptly turned them away without any discussion as it was difficult enough living in the area with people behaving like this. A person called the police days later and said that he had placed the bag as bait to catch mulloway fish and the police accepted this. The timing of this action was very coincidental with the announcement of the location of the life saving facility and the baiting behaviour was uncommon, this being the only known incident of this kind in over twelve years that I lived in the area. These events scared my wife and I. Most local people had a belief they knew who was responsible for this act. Later, on another occasion when we publicised a club barbeque in Eros Reserve we woke on the morning to find the area littered with smelly blood and bone fertilizer. This was strategically located in piles around the picnic tables and activity area in the park. Another local removed council beach signage that he did not like and buried the signs in the sand dunes one night. This person was very quick to complain about anyone or anything yet he conducted his poor behaviour under the cover of dark, despite holding himself to be an upstanding member of the community.

Chapter 4
A Time For Reflection

The best location for a surf life saving club in Mandurah was a central location at Town Beach or Halls Head, however the Town Beach area had been redeveloped by the government agency LandCorp around 2000 as a marina and final planning unfortunately did not cater for surf life saving clubrooms. Council now advised that they had other plans for the Halls Head foreshore area where the abandoned yacht club building stood. There were two surf life saving clubs in Mandurah from December 2003, one at each end of the broader Mandurah area, being Port Bouvard and San Remo, with San Remo being more connected to central Mandurah. One large strong club in Mandurah with two wings north and south was floated with council in the early days but was not taken seriously. The two wings could have patrolled each side of town and provided a platform for competition and service delivery from one strong single base. Rockingham Council a larger adjoining council has one surf life saving club with a main patrol area and other areas that have outpost patrols, whilst Perth with a population of around 2 million has 12 clubs and Mandurah with a population of 80,683 (June 2013) source "City's Profile – Mandurah Council" has 2 clubs.

A comparison of Mandurah with other regional centres and clubs in WA such as Geraldton and Bunbury shows two clubs in each town, one club being larger, more dominant and older than the other. Both towns have a long history with Surf Life Saving, Bunbury Surf Life Saving Club was founded in 1915 and Geraldton in 1930.

A historic look at other clubs reveals, club 19 in WA is Yanchep, founded in 1991, the Two-Rocks Yanchep area has a population of fewer than 5,000 people. Clubs 14 through to 18 are Mullaloo commenced 1960, Secret Harbour 1981, Quinns Mindarie 1982, Broome 1988 and Esperance Goldfields during 1990. Club 21 is Binningup founded in 2002 with a shared clubroom that was completed in 2007. Binningup has a population of less than 1000. Mandurah is club 20 founded in 1996. Coogee was founded in 2003 and clubroom construction at a cost of over $10 million commenced in 2012 whilst the club had adequate temporary club rooms prior to this and the club had great support from its council. Six surf life saving clubs commenced in 2003, Dongara Denison, Margaret River, Dalyellup, Champion Bay, Coogee and Port Bouvard. This was a prolific time in the development of surf life saving clubs in WA. No clubs formed from 1960 through until 1981 and the period during 2003 certainly made up for that dormant era.

History will show that in Mandurah a locality that has two surf life saving clubs, that the youngest one was granted clubrooms in one of the shortest timeframes and the older one waited one of the longest timeframes for club rooms in WA.

The Mandurah Yacht Club in Halls Head became vacant in 2000 with the development of the Marina on the opposite side of the estuary mouth and this building would have suited a surf life saving club. I approached various councillors and council staff and requested use of this building in the interim during 2004 with an unconditional club guarantee that the club would move out within a month when an alternate use was found for the building. The club could have managed the building and hired the function section to the community so as to generate income and provide a community meeting place. The building was functional for a surf life saving club with a lookout tower included. This proposal was ignored by council after initial interest was shown. The old Mandurah Yacht Club building is shown below.

Old Yacht Club

The yacht club building remained with little use for many years, and has been used intermittently by various clubs for storage and other groups for functions. Our club had storage at the facility for a number of years. Council finally asked us to move all our equipment out in 2010 and offered the club use of an old sea container on the beach in Halls Head for storage. I queried the safety of this option and staff replied that it was safe and we could use it until our club house was built. We did use the container until the club house was built, however we lost an inflatable rescue boat, that cost around $14,000 new, that was stored in the container. In later years council allowed development of a storage shed adjacent to the yacht club building for other water based clubs and the main building still did not have a permanent occupant when this book was published.

Issues with Surf Life Saving

During 2005 I became president of the club and had been busy applying to SLSWA and other institutions for equipment grants for a vehicle and new inflatable rescue boat. I had applied on behalf of the club for a Yamaha Grant amongst other grants, for two pieces of equipment with the grant being under the control of Surf Life Saving WA. I thought that we submitted a good case to be considered then heard nothing other than we were not successful. I set about investigating who was on the grant panel and which club had received the equipment. To my surprise I was advised that the grant panel was dominated by personnel who were current or past members of a large Perth city club and that club was awarded the equipment. I raised this with SLSWA management via a letter and was asked to withdraw the letter, which I refused to do. After much discussion a senior person in the organisation suggested that I apply for another similar grant in a few months. Our club was then successful obtaining a Yamaha Rhino vehicle and new inflatable rescue boat hull. However the club had to source another sponsor to pay half the cost of the vehicle. The Land Developer at Madora Bay provided this for the club without fuss. SLSWA staff requested a meeting with me to query who would be responsible for the equipment and if we had adequate storage for the equipment. They were shown my garage and left without further comment. This was the start of easier more enjoyable times at our club on the beach, but we had challenges ahead with respect to building our home.

Surf Life Saving WA had staff that were well connected to committee members from Port Bouvard Surf Life Saving Club. They were long time members from the same Perth club. The friendship and life saving service together was spoken about on various occasions. Surf life savers tend to develop an emotional attachment to their club of origin and its members. It is crucial that you have the full support of your state body and your council when establishing a surf life saving club. Councils will not act without your state body's support. We would learn later that our club would not be in a home before Port Bouvard contrary to what council officers had said to our club in 2004.

During 2005 our club was elevated again from a probationary club to an affiliated club of Surf Life Saving WA. This was another significant milestone when the Board of Directors of Surf Life Saving WA voted to re-admit Mandurah as an affiliated club. The club had previously been an affiliated club before going into recession in 2002. We would later feel that affiliation did not carry great meaning for our council and the state body when a probationary club was promoted before us to have a clubhouse in our district.

A few years later in 2007 we learned that Port Bouvard Surf Life Saving Club, a probationary club, had received all the financial support they required to have their building commence. Affiliated clubs should hold higher status in the organisation. When we heard this I sent an email to an officer at the Mandurah Council asking why affiliation of our surf life saving club did not carry greater weight in their approval process for a clubhouse as they had granted a probationary club of SLSAW a building before our affiliated club. This email was forwarded directly on to Management of SLSWA. Two things followed, I was berated and affiliation for Port Bouvard was rushed through.

The Surf Life Saving WA constitution had been amended prior to these events. An amendment to governance had taken power away from WA Club Presidents and bestowed it with management of the organisation. Management could now make decisions without consulting with the President of SLSWA and the clubs of WA. Various committees and sub committees were also set up to feed back into the organisation. This change to governance was not welcomed by some with long standing experience in the organisation and was not properly understood by others. No review has been undertaken since to understand its success or failures. Change is a good thing, however review and ongoing monitoring is as important. This amendment can provide a reason among others why Mandurah's building started to take second place.

Another reason why our club was now being placed second in the process for a building was, we had heard, that the developer at Port Bouvard had provided the council with a contribution of around $200,000 for an ablution building at Pyramids Beach and council had not constructed the facility. There were no ablutions at Pyramids Beach and building a Surf Life Saving Club at Port Bouvard would also bring public ablutions. An official of the land development company held a committee position at Port Bouvard SLSC during the development period of that club. Port Bouvard SLSC had a short development period before gaining its club house and its rapid development meant that there were some occasions when a deviation from standards occurred.

During 2006 our club and Port Bouvard SLSC jointly arranged a nipper carnival at Port Bouvard Surf Life Saving Club. The carnival was due to start at 9 am so I had arrived at 8.45 am with our gear and other members from our club to find that there were very few people and no surf life savers at their beach. At that time all surf life saving clubs would sign on for patrols over a two way radio with a command centre known as Surf Com in Perth and provide details of patrol capabilities and beach conditions. Port Bouvard Club was the first club in the southern metro region to be called and it would then be Mandurah and onwards up the coast to the northern beaches of Perth. I had taken one of our five hand held radios to the carnival to monitor the crew that was on duty at our beach and provide assistance if required.

At 9 am a few more nippers and their parents had arrived at Port Bouvard, however their surf life saving patrol was not on the beach.

A few minutes later Surf Com called them and to my astonishment there was a reply stating that they were on the beach with a full patrol and a summary of beach conditions was provided that was a little incorrect. I had turned the volume up and other people around me heard the transmission. Surf Com continued through to all the other clubs and finally at about 9.20 am their patrol members and equipment started arriving. Their patrol members were a little agitated when they saw I had a hand held radio and I queried the transmission that was made while not at the beach. They later said that they had been at a function the night before and the call was made from a home where the club stored their gear. This was not the best behaviour from a developing club in our organisation, an organisation that has a long proud history of keeping beaches safe. I raised this with management at Surf Life Saving the following week and there was little interest shown.

Port Bouvard club stored gear at their President's home before they had facilities and the club payed a storage fee for this. It was disclosed as "Storage Fee (Yeulba)" in their annual report. Yeulba Street, Falcon was a street where their president rented a home and the financial amount in the annual report equated to about $180 per week over a year. This was not widely understood and I have not seen other clubs do anything similar.

My queries with our organisation about standards not being followed and the probationary club status versus affiliated club status would see me on the wrong side of some. I was of the opinion that if standards were set then all should follow them and if not the governing body should have the gumption to step in and maintain their standards equitably.

On another occasion we held a fundraising event in the Mandurah Recreation Centre and offered half the proceeds to Port Bouvard Surf Life Saving Club. The cash raised was promptly collected by a senior person from their club and we never heard any more or received thanks and the gesture was never reciprocated. We did also arrange a joint funding grant with Port Bouvard SLSC from the Department of Sports and Recreation (DSR) that required proper acquittal by both club. DSR would not provide a grant to our club only and they required this joint arrangement, despite our objection. We acquitted the grant in accordance with the agreement but Port Bouvard SLSC did not and we were held partly responsible for their actions and hence this style of joint work was too difficult to continue. I continued to hold out an olive branch to the Port Bouvard Club contrary to what other committee members of our club were telling me. I think I should have taken more notice of their comments.

2007 was The Year of The Surf Life Saver, a commemoration of 100 years of surf life saving in Australia. There was a long build up to the commemoration and many events were planned for the year. One event was a morning tea with the Prime Minister John Howard at Scarboro Surf Life Saving Club. Presidents of WA clubs were invited and I accepted for Mandurah. There was a security screening process conducted via the police as a prerequisite. I had left for Perth the afternoon before for business meetings and stayed overnight. I happened to talk to an employee from Surf Life Saving WA late in the day prior to the morning tea and said to him that I would see him at the event. He advised that I was not on the list and that I had no security clearance to attend. I was annoyed as I had accepted the invite and taken time out to go to Perth. I strongly expressed my disappointment and was advised the next morning by SLSWA that I had clearance to attend. It was great that I could be involved with the organisation in such activities and that I could feel like I was part of the broader surf life saving community.

Another area where inclusion was not the best was the Peel Area Support Operations, Jet Ski Rescue Team. The Peel area encompasses the broader area of Mandurah. The local rescue team was made up of members from Secret Harbour SLSC with one outsider for many years, and the group is based at Secret Harbour. Secret Harbour is just north of the Peel Region and Mandurah is centre of the region. In an emergency in Mandurah, Mandurah members would hold the best local knowledge and response times. Mandurah members were not adequately encouraged or properly informed so applications for the group were not submitted. During the 2013 intake Mandurah did not received all the application documents until one hour after the deadline had closed. As a result no applications were sent due to the uncertainty created. Mandurah SLSC had one member accepted into the group in 2014 and two more in 2015 which was great for inclusion in this mobile response group.

During early discussions regarding the location of our club in 2004 SLSWA had told council that Mandurah would need to be a mobile club due to its vast coastline with swimmers that dispersed themselves along beaches and that water craft including jet skis would be equipment required for the club to operate effectively. Council business plans as a result included development of a mobile surf life saving presence jointly with our club on the vast northern beaches of Mandurah using water craft. Council business plans also make reference to building a mobile patrol with our club for Town Beach which is 5 kilometres away from San Remo. It was difficult for the club to effectively build this plan without the required mobile craft.

The WA State Premier announced around 2010 that every surf life saving club in WA would receive a jet ski through funds from the state government, to improve beach patrols after a number of shark attacks. The local state government member queried where our jet ski was in November 2013 during a visit to the club as he was aware of the undertaking. A SLSWA owned jet ski was finally based at our club in November 2014. Training operators and growing capable volunteer personnel takes time. SLSWA retain ownership of all surf life saving jet skis in the state and they were run somewhat independently of clubs in a support and emergency role, while drawing personnel from clubs until 2016 when the jet ski model was changed.

The State President of SLSWA also made a public announcement at an event in Secret Harbour that every club would have an emergency response device for remote use on outlying or remote areas at club beaches. Mandurah with vast beaches is a classic club for such devices and we received a number of queries about the whereabouts of the device that our organisation had publicly advised would be in use on Mandurah beaches. We never received this device despite asking for it on numerous occasions and each year we would be asked where our device was by SLSWA communication maintenance personnel, as it was due for its annual service. I eventually tracked our device down and it had been given to one of the larger Perth clubs.

A survey undertaken by SLSWA in 2015 on issues confronting clubs highlighted six areas. Among them were volunteer recognition and workload issues for volunteers. A similar study was undertaken years earlier by different staff in the organisation and similar issues were apparent. Will the organisation resolve these issues?

Chapter 5

Riding on a Wave

The 2005/06 season was probably one of our best in terms of steps forward without a clubhouse, when our turnover, membership numbers and equipment increased fivefold. San Remo had also been approved in 2005 as the site for our proposed club house. Our club had also won gold medals and various other medals at the State Junior and Masters Championships. We won third place in the Club of The Year Award and Administrator of The Year at the Surf Life Saving WA Awards of Excellence at the end of the season. Membership was well over 200 and it was difficult running the club from people's homes with most of the non beach activity and equipment based at my house in Ormsby Terrace near the proposed club location.

Nominations for the awards of excellence culminated in an interview of the finalists at the offices of Surf Life Saving WA. It was agreed that I would go as Club President along with Kirk Bamford an ex-school principal from Canada who had joined our club a few years earlier. We had trained Kirk who was fit and keen to be one of our best surf life savers and engaged him in many club activities. During the interview I was questioned about the club and our recent growth which I was very familiar with and answered well for the first 15 to 20 minutes. When questions about training, education and member retention started I was a somewhat lost and Kirk took control and did an excellent job with his responses. The winner that year was Mullaloo, second Secret Harbour and Mandurah was third.

in the news

Mandurah on crest of a wave

MANDURAH Surf Lifesaving Club performed well at this month's 2006 Surf Life Saving Western Australia Awards of Excellence, attracting two major gongs.

The awards were held on May 20 at the Esplanade Hotel in Fremantle, where the Mandurah club was one of five finalists for the Club of the Year award from 27 eligible WA clubs.

Mandurah placed third, behind Secret Harbour Surf Lifesaving Club and winner Mullaloo Surf Lifesaving Club, the latter of which is also National Club of the Year.

Mandurah club secretary-treasurer Mercedes Barrie won the Administrator of the Year Award, beating four other finalists in the category.

The awards celebrate achievements and growth in surf lifesaving during the previous season and recognise the contributions of club members in helping the local community.

The Mandurah club has also done well at the SLSWA State Country Championships, picking up two gold medals in the junior competition and three bronze in the masters category.

Mandurah Surf Lifesaving Club members Mercedes Barrie, Kirk Bamford, Jake Webb, Georgina Webb and Warwick Webb. *Picture: Daniel Wilkins*

Coastal Times 31 May 2006

During the season I had also got together with the presidents of Secret Harbour Surf Life Saving Club, Max Hannah, and Coogee Surf Life Saving, Club Daryl Smith and we set up the first club alliance in WA known as the Southern Beaches Alliance. This was done to boost the strength of our smaller clubs, to share and improve training, ideas, resources, boost purchasing power, improve sponsorship and promote joint club sponsorship while also promoting surf life saving in the region with dedicated areas and operating terms agreed for each club. Surf Life Saving WA was notified and the clubs met on an annual basis. The door was left open to include Port Bouvard Surf Life Saving Club when they reached affiliation with Surf Life Saving WA, however it was a number of years after their affiliation that they were included when a new president of Port Bouvard, Damian Mahony and I formalised the alliance with the other clubs. This alliance originally led to the formation of the local area carnivals by SLSWA as a feeder/qualifier for the annual surf life saving state championships. Mandurah and Port Bouvard Clubs formed a closer bond when Port Bouvard was under the leadership of Damian Mahony, but unfortunately he suddenly resigned from the club during the 2011/12 season and this rebuilding of the relationship fell away for a while after his departure.

The alliance was productive for our small club and we gained great support from the two larger clubs, which promoted growth in our club and helped with success. Max Hannah and Daryl Smith offered excellent support to me and our club for many years.

Secret Harbour SLSC was a club that we enjoyed joint sponsorship with in a simple cooperative fashion in the early days. We attended some of their events and had fun times. At one of their functions that six members from Mandurah attended, we set a challenge to return to our club with as many of their awards and gear as possible. By the end of the night we had their club flag, a couple of major trophies and a few other bits and pieces. I had possession of one of their flags at the event and was caught by one of their life members Billy dropping another one down, when he yelled, "What are you doing?" I replied that his people had asked me to change it for the other one that I had in my possession. He promptly walked off. We all returned to my house later that evening and then began texting and emailing them pictures of our booty. Their guys played along with us for about a week, until I agreed to drop the gear off at one of their member's homes and was told that I would be met by the surf boat crew for pay back. I did get a little nervous but showed up and Wayne took the gear and offered me a beer. I was invited to more events but a close eye was kept on me for a few years. This is the style of humorous taunting that clubs should enjoy while also respecting and supporting each other.

(Left to right Warwick Webb, Barbara & Kirk Bamford, Michael White & Georgina Webb)

Our success had turned the spotlight on us in both positive and negative ways. Surf life savers are required to undertake an annual assessment or requalification of skills. Generally this assessment should be undertaken by an independent assessor from another club. Later in 2006 at the beginning of the 2006/07 season we had asked the president of Pt Bouvard club to undertake our assessments as he was a registered assessor. We had our members, who included a group of new younger surf life savers, prepared and we all set about doing our tasks. The assessor was dictatorial and focused on our juniors, telling them they were not competent. Unfortunately, I became aware after damage had been done and I pulled him to one side with another assessor who was helping and suggested that he should send them back for further training before classing them as incompetent. The discussion became a little tense and I eventually asked him to leave. The other assessor promptly completed and passed all who remained as they were competent. Unfortunately damage was done and some young club members left the beach and did not return to the club or surf life saving as their esteem had been damaged.

Running a successful club requires growth in membership, fundraising and activities for members to be involved in. We instigated an arrangement with the council whereby we would have a beach cleanup day at the commencement of the season, then continue each Sunday while on patrol monitoring and removing rubbish along the northern beaches of Mandurah. Council contributed $600 annually towards this and arranged rubbish pickup, bags and gloves on the cleanup day. In the first three years we removed a large amount of rubbish annually including furniture, tyres, building material, knives, bottles, wooden objects, boat parts and many other items that could cause harm. It was a way of accident prevention while also improving cleanliness on our beaches and fundraising for the club. It is noticeable how rubbish reduces when the beaches are clean and people are then more compelled to use bins.

Club members at beach cleanup October 2008

The Madora Progress Association did acknowledge the beach cleanup work we did in their newsletter of February 2007 in an article headed "Bouquets to the San Remo Surf Club".

> "On a Sunday morning about a month ago whilst some of our residents were enjoying a morning's fishing, a yellow beach buggy ventured along the beach. First reaction was annoyance as vehicles are not allowed on our beach; so it was a wonderful surprise to discover the two young folk in the buggy were actually picking up all the rubbish, left by thoughtless folk, as they slowly drove along. Written on the vehicle was "Surf Lifesaving" (who for obvious reasons) are permitted to drive on the beach. The following two Sundays the rubbish collection occurred again. Fantastic! Let's extend a huge THANK YOU to the club and appreciate this asset which benefits our young people and the community."

After such a successful 2005/06 season we had a club vehicle, boat, trailer, rescue and training equipment, club records, documents and a computer at my house. My two kids would play in the back yard among an array of club gear. One day in late 2006 my 6 year old daughter rode her bicycle into the inflatable rescue boat trailer and injured herself. This made me realise that having the club gear at my house was not ideal. I set about approaching the council and Surf Life Saving WA to seek assistance for storage for club equipment. I explored ideas to set up a storage shed in the park versus on a privately owned lot. A person at Surf Life Saving WA offered to help me build a plan to take to council for the storage shed. In an email on 21 November 2006 he stated "If you wish to arrange a time to meet council and we can collectively work up a strategy to present to the council, I am more than happy to work through this." I accepted his offer and set a date for the meeting in Mandurah. I took time off from work and he did not arrive. This person did apologise in April 2007 with an excuse that I had gone on holidays so the issue had fallen off his radar. His help was never provided on this issue. Council staff offered very little assistance despite requests. Eventually a year later and after many hours of my time, and numerous road blocks I had approval to erect a storage shed in Eros Reserve, San Remo for club equipment.

We had requested assistance financial or otherwise from the council and received no financial support towards the shed. They had even tried to charge us an $800 annual fee for a shed that we built after it was erected. We had to have this fee overturned at a full council meeting with more bureaucracy consuming volunteer time. The club had also requested that council help by providing a wash down tap at the ablution building in Eros Reserve as gear had been washed at my home for years. It took over two years and many requests to get the tap from council. Council did not contribute towards our beach patrol services that helped keep council controlled beaches safer and it was a struggle getting almost any assistance from them on an operations level. Setting up a beach patrol with vehicle, boat, first aid facilities and many other items requires equipment to the value of over $60,000 and at least six trained life savers. All of this was self funded by the club.

We raised $7,000 for a shed with the help of Mandurah Rotary Clubs by holding a quiz night. Alcoa of Australia offered us a grant that provided $3,000 and 10 employees for 4 hours of club work. We used the 10 employees to pave the floor after the shed was constructed. A shed supplier offered us a shed at cost, the club paid for site works and Alcoa's contribution paid for the floor.

Shed builders recall a nearby resident approaching them and being difficult during construction, however they just moved on with the task. All the equipment except the vehicle, surf boat, a surf ski, administration documents and laptop filled the 65 square metre shed. Nearby residents had requested that the vehicle stay at my home as it would be a target for vandals as the shed did not have power therefore no monitored security.

Shed in Eros Reserve that the club called home from 2007 until 2013

A nearby track that was left from a beach groyne construction in 2005 lead to the beach so vehicle access was good and we placed the shed in a location that would allow it to stay when the clubhouse was eventually built. The groyne had been constructed to reduce beach erosion. A parcel of land adjacent to Eros Reserve known as lot 106 was a lot that had been partly swallowed up by the ocean overtime and it was still privately owned. The land was required for construction of the groyne and later the club building. In 2004 council contacted the elderly owner who had many years of outstanding rates on this unusable lot that was half in the ocean and half in the dunes. The owner agreed to hand the lot back to the state if the outstanding rates were written off. Agreement was reached which allowed construction of a groyne and later the club.

During the lead up to construction of the main club building in 2011 council endeavoured to claim that they had helped with construction of the shed. An article was written by council for the press claiming that they had helped with shed construction and it was provided to me for review. Luckily I stopped it as such incorrect claims would have infuriated me and others, knowing the battle we had experienced to build the shed.

I did not renominate for club president at the end of the 2007 season as 12 months of negotiating with the council to locate our shed on Eros Reserve with no help from SLSWA had worn me down. Our state body had let me down in various other ways. They have an event sanctioning process for clubs wishing to provide help to other organisations for community or sports events, or to conduct carnivals. They had been difficult to deal with during sanctioning. We had helped various local events, sporting carnivals and council when water safety was needed. An annual swim known as the Cambria Island Swim required water safety and I submitted an event application to SLSWA in November 2006 for this event that was to be held in February 2007. I informed the event organisers that I would arrange water safety if the event was sanctioned by SLSWA. Many hours of planning, working with event organisers and risk mitigation are required for such events which I had happily provided. Proper planning and preparation will result in smooth events without incidents. In all the events that I provided water safety for, there were never any unforseen or dangerous incidents.

Our state body provided no feedback after the application for the Cambria Island Swim was submitted. The event organiser required time for an alternate plan if we did not get approval. I had queried our state body numerous times both verbally and in emails for feedback and four days before the event had words with them as the event organiser was very anxious and there was no time to arrange an alternate plan. This was not ideal if our approval was not forth coming at such a late stage. The approval came through a few days before the event leaving us all short of time and stressed before finalising our plans for a large potentially risky swim. Volunteers had been let down again by paid people.

On other occasions SLSWA asked us to arrange water safety for an ocean surf ski race and they also requested that we man a barbeque at the end of the race. In return they offered the club $500 plus costs. It took many months and repeated requests to finally have them honour their agreement. On another occasion they borrowed our only rescue boat and returned to Perth with some of the boat equipment. We waited weeks for the equipment to be returned to us while also having to use the boat. All these events that are small to some do demoralise and wear down a volunteer who also holds a job, has a family and many other commitments. Our local event assistance in the water safety area was gradually reduced, leaving council, sporting bodies and other groups without this service due to these difficulties.

When I announced that I would not continue as president I prepared a simple memorandum of understanding between the club,

SLSWA and council to document our understanding of the future for development of our club for the benefit of new comers. Council showed initial interest in signing the document, but neither party was willing to progress with the memorandum of understanding.

We had encouraged other club members to nominate for club president towards the end of the 2006/07 season and all were reluctant due to the work load in the club while also dealing with facility approval and development. Finally, just before the annual general meeting in mid 2007 Andrew Harrison agreed to take the role if I stayed on as vice president, which I did. I continued doing some of the work that I had previously undertaken and Andrew liaised with the bodies that had previously let me down. As a volunteer giving time endlessly to undertake on occasion unnecessary tasks provided by paid people or to be let down or not supported by them when you could be spending time with your family or dealing with other commitments, diminishes the enthusiasm towards volunteerism. Being president of a club is one task and development of a club facility is another large role. Presidents of large organisations or clubs are often experienced figureheads with support. However in a small developing group the president's role is different and it is often very hands on with the president also undertaking a large portion of the work.

Andrew successfully completed one year as president and did not wish to remain in the role. Andrew remained in the club for a few more years until his children lost interest, however he still shows an interest in club activities and remains in contact with us. The following year my wife Georgina took on the club president's role and I stayed on as vice president. Georgina was employed by council as a marketing officer and her manager was also the council appointed person to handle club matters and development of our clubhouse. This mix would prove difficult for her and resulted in Georgina taking 6 months unpaid leave from work to manage her health as events were starting to take their toll on her in the second half of her term. I covered her role during this period. I was approached by a number of business folk and surf life saving people in town who suggested that I should renominate for club president again as I had the background and the determination not to let Mandurah Council or SLSWA walk away from our project or prolong it any further. I took this advice and became president again from 2009 until 2012 and was happy to leave the role again once construction had begun.

During a council meeting about progress or lack of it for our club facility which was attended by others from our club and Surf Life Saving WA, an engineer from the council who was new in the role tried to defend an unreasonable council executive. I promptly turned on him and told him that he was new in town and that he was unaware of all the background, therefore he should not defend someone without understanding the issue. He remained quiet for the rest of the meeting and over time I developed respect for him as a decent person with good intentions who thanked volunteers for their efforts in the community, and who approached issues pragmatically on most occasions. This meeting was not one that I was proud of but it allowed me to get a few things off my chest during frustrating times.

During 2008 Georgina and I started having doubts that our club facility would ever be built as our progress was being stalled and Port Bouvard's club house seemed to be the focus for our council and others. This focus and attention meant that Port Bouvard Surf Life Saving Club a smaller younger club than ours started gaining momentum and eventually took over as the larger club in town and started spreading into territory that was traditionally ours. They began seeking sponsors and members in our backyard while also holding fundraising events in our territory. A few of their committee members were overzealous and happy to tread on toes. These actions created friction between the clubs again.

I later initiated a memorandum of understanding between the two clubs which set ground rules and areas for the two clubs so as to avoid conflict as uncontrolled conflict would turn sponsors and people away. The two clubs agreed to meet annually to review the agreement. In 2012 both clubs met and agreed on the coming season, including collection areas for annual street appeal and sponsor allocation. It was agreed that our club would collect at the train station among other locations on annual street appeal day. When our members arrived at the train station so did Port Bouvard members contrary to our agreement. Their members eventually left after discussions with us and their board of management. There were other sponsor issues that we dealt with delicately. Our club followed street appeal day rules which stated the hours of collection, approvals and venues for collection. Surf life savers from other clubs were seen collecting out of hours in licensed premises contrary to rules. Conduct and following your word and undertakings are important for any successful organisation.

In January 2012 I organised a skills session with four Australian Iron men and women at Town Beach and offered 30 places to Port Bouvard club which they accepted. Two days before the event the Port Bouvard president declined our offer leaving very short notice for us to fill the places, another let down for club relations. The event went off well with great skills passed on in a friendly atmosphere and a few of our young girls took some time to forget the images of fit professional ironmen in Speedos on our beach.

Chapter 6

Worried About The Future

2008 was the beginning of another difficult time for the club, doubt about what the future held was often discussed. Local media were interested in our plight and they endeavoured to engage us and others on the issue. A few articles appeared in the local press during the year.

The article in the *Mandurah Mail* 14 August 2008 raised concerns about our future and one of our members queried why a junior probationary club had been placed before us for a club building. Journalists quoted the CEO of the council who stated that "funding applications were submitted for Port Bouvard on the basis of land availability on which a facility could be built". This comment was made over three years after the council had approved San Remo as the site for our club. The council had then taken nearly two years to submit an application to amend their management order over the site, an amendment that should have taken less than a year. The management order had been vested with the council since 1978. The CEO went on to say that the

"City is committed to the needs of both surf life saving clubs as both clubs are important service providers within Mandurah with equally important needs for facilities."

Surf club worried about the future

by **Holly Freitag**

AS THE fight to build a clubhouse continues for the Mandurah Surf Life Saving Club, its management is uncertain about the club's future.

As one of Western Australia's oldest surf life saving clubs without a facility, members and management said it was frustrating to be fighting for a clubhouse after more than 12 years.

Club administrator Mercedes Barrie said it was "disheartening" to see younger surf life saving clubs allocated funding for a clubhouse before them.

She said it was difficult to attract finance for their long-awaited facility.

"We don't know our future because we have no facilities to offer," Ms Barrie said.

The members currently operate from a self-funded shed on Eros Reserve in San Remo, a site that was approved for a surf life saving facility in 2005.

The club needs funding to build the clubhouse, but has been unsuccessful in attracting money for many years.

With the shed due to be pulled down in two years due to planning approval requirements, the club is questioning where they will go from there.

Ms Barrie said it was difficult to offer members activities throughout winter as there was no clubhouse to operate from.

The Mandurah Surf Life Saving Club was eager to find out why Port Bouvard surf life saving club, a younger and then probationary club, was granted funding before them.

Mandurah City chief executive Mark Newman said funding applications were submitted for Port Bouvard on the basis of land availability on which a facility could be built.

It was then revealed to the *Mandurah Mail* that Mandurah City has ownership over the land in San Remo by way of management order, which has been in place since 1978.

The management order over Eros Reserve, on Orestes Street, states that the power to lease "shall be for the purpose of facilitating the development and management of a surf lifesaving club". It was last vested to and revoked from the City in 2007 to accommodate an amendment.

"The City is committed to the needs of both surf life saving clubs as both clubs are important service providers within Mandurah with equally important needs for facilities," Mr Newman said. "We want to build appropriate multi-purpose facilities in both locations that serve both the needs of the surf life saving clubs and the wider community."

Surf Life Saving WA (SLS WA) chief executive Paul Andrews said the Mandurah club was still waiting for approvals of the designated land being vested back to the city.

Mr Andrews said SLS WA was trying to find as much money as they could for the Mandurah club. He said SLS WA ranked the club's funding application to the Sport and Recreation Department's Community Sport and Recreation Facilities Fund highly last year.

Unfortunately the club was knocked back for funding approval.

"It's an ongoing issue and just a matter of getting funding, I'm more than happy to assist (the club)," Mr Andrews said.

Mr Newman said there were currently more than 40 sporting and community groups in Mandurah seeking new or upgraded facilities. He said the total cost of this infrastructure program was more than $60 million.

"The City of Mandurah, along with Surf Life Saving WA, used the (2007) Year of the Life Saver to promote the community service contribution of both clubs and the need for facilities," Mr Newman said. He said at least five years was expected between identifying the need for a facility and the delivery of an operational venue.

Mandurah Mail 14 August 2008

The CEO of SLSWA was also interviewed by journalists and was quoted in the article as saying "the Mandurah club was still waiting for approvals of the designated land being vested back to the city". He went on to say that "I am more than happy to assist (the club)." These comments made in August 2008 also appeared odd as the management order for the land was vested with council in 1978 with an amendment in 2007 that was for the purpose of facilitating the development and management of a surf life saving club within lot 2723.

We did take up the assistance offer and got attendance at one meeting at the council then unfortunately the person was always busy when meetings arose. The message from SLSWA to us was then portrayed that they had paved the way for us when they had helped Port Bouvard SLSC through their process ahead of ours. This seemed to be a polite way of saying that they were not too interested in helping. Both council and SLSWA stated on various occasions that both clubs would be treated equally. Equity to us in this regard seemed to be a low priority when we considered these actions.

Another article in the local press covered a story about the council's charter, stating how they should be working to build communities and encourage volunteerism. However their actions were doing the opposite to our club in that member retention and credibility was difficult when a junior breakaway group of our club was placed before us. The lack of help and difficulties posed had also resulted in problems with member retention. I recall one of our members, Gary, who had located to Mandurah from an eastern seaboard club with 25 years of surf life saving experience who assumed the role of vice president for a short time. Gary attended a number of council meetings with me and later suggested that the lack of support from our council was intolerable, and that it would unfortunately take a drowning on our beaches for things to change. As a result he did not wish to stay on the committee, but remained as a club member for a few years training people in surf boat rowing before finally leaving surf life saving. Gary was familiar with councils assisting and helping eastern states surf life saving clubs in all facets of their operations in a true partnership. In his words "they would treat you like gold for the volunteer work you did on their beaches."

Shortly after these articles were published I received a phone call one evening from a lady, Donna Selby, who had read the articles after recently moving to Mandurah. She had a background in grant applications, and relatives who had been involved with surf life saving. I promptly met with her and we engaged her to assist us with grants on a type of success fee arrangement. There were many late nights preparing grant applications for Lotterywest and again for the Department of Sport and Recreation (DSR). Council had assisted us with the first DSR grant application, however we now had Donna assist us with round two. A council manager would not provide us with all the information from the first application that we required and he was being difficult to deal with. I called a meeting with council and requested attendance of their CEO. He declined, so I telephoned him and requested his attendance, telling him that his staffers were being somewhat difficult and his presence would overcome these difficulties. He did not sound keen about attending however to our surprise and the surprise of the manager he turned up when we were all in the room about to commence the meeting. His attendance helped our position, and he asked the manager to support us and provide all the information that we required. He did also say during the meeting that council could have done a better job in some areas with our club development. The next day the information was provided to us and Donna set to work with Georgina and Mercedes Barrie the club secretary/treasurer and myself.

Council had prepared most of Port Bouvard's grants, however not in our case and the equal treatment for both clubs was evaporating.

We would also finally end up raising more than Port Bouvard did in funds towards our building without any adjustments by the council for our extra contribution to keep equity in the process. I recall the nights before these two grants were due and the candle was being burned at both ends to produce documents each about an inch thick. Luckily they both just made it on time.

We had applied for Department of Sports and Recreation funding in 2008 for our proposed building and we were unsuccessful. During this application a council staffer in the recreation department told us again that our building project was not her pet project and nominated another one that was. We did not have a chance as we had been ranked number three out of various other projects. People politics, personal preferences and opinions from people in control unfortunately have a large influence on some decisions. It seemed to some in town that council and our state body were not serious about our project and there was a chance that it could be lost.

Grant documents require supporting material from various people and bodies including local authorities, politicians and state or industry bodies to show support for a viable project. Politicians are usually very accommodating if the project is a good one, but unfortunately others are not always as willing and I recall requesting a letter of support four times from our state body for one of the grants and having to write a draft for them a few days before it was due in an endeavour to encourage them to oblige.

Time then marched by and we heard nothing, and the mood became dull. I recall in April 2009 talking to my wife Georgina when we agreed that we had both had about enough of fighting for this facility. It was affecting our lives too much and we should seriously consider giving up. I went to work the next day and Georgina telephoned me, she was ecstatic with the news that Lotterywest had approved our grant for $450,000 towards the building. This great news renewed our determination and we agreed to continue on.

It was only a few days later that an officer from the Department of Sports and Recreation called me in the morning to advise that we had also been successful with their grant for $888,000 and that an announcement would be made in a few hours. He asked me to hold off telling too many people until it was officially announced which I did, however I called Georgina and told her. She then went and told her manger who was also our club liaison person in the council. He promptly replied that this was a problem and that we had created a problem with our success. He also had his nose out of joint as we had the news prior to the grant being announced or council being informed. I later challenged him as I had been in the room when Port Bouvard SLSC received their grant monies for their building and he and other council people had congratulated them. I queried why he was not treating us equally as had been promised previously and he did not reply. We never received his congratulations nor, unfortunately did the equal treatment with respect to grant preparation from the council eventuate.

These grants all came with conditions, a use by date and an acquittal process. These dates were based around information supplied by the council on timeframes as they ultimately owned the land and therefore the process and they would also own the building when it was constructed. Council timelines would cause us a few problems as council could not stick to them and multiple extensions would be required down the track, with one of the grant providers also later giving us a final deadline to use the money by. Despite our great fund raising efforts Council had control with regard to approvals and other requirements to start the project as it was their project on their land and they called the shots. Council had experience at these dealings as they had completed projects similar to this one and we had not. The final grant deadline may have helped us in that it finally forced commencement of the project as council would have lost credibility if our grant monies for the project were lost due to their inaction. The first grant was drawn down over three years after it was awarded.

Funding for the project would ultimately be provided by State Government bodies, with the balance of $450,000 from Lotterywest and around $700,000 from council. We did spend many hours on Federal Government Grants and also lobbied federal government politicians. In the early days we had a federal labour leader as our vice patron and I would later meet with his replacement on numerous occasions. I recall one meeting in 2008 when after much discussion on our plight he calmly suggested that I was wasting my f__ken time and that I should give it away. It left me a little shocked but I later realised that I should have given him away rather as he did not help us other than provide lip service. I did meet with him on numerous other occasions over the following years. We sent him a letter expressing our disappointment about the federal government's lack of support in 2012 but also left the door open for them to return to the table for future funding. We did not hear from him.

This federal government minister, who I had engaged regarding our funding, made promises of substantial funding for rebuilding Secret Harbour SLSC during the 2013 election.

Port Bouvard Surf Life Saving Club was granted around $500,000 from the federal government for their clubhouse through a grant influenced by a member of the Howard Liberal government shortly before they lost office. This decision would be placed under review by the incoming Rudd Labor government in 2009 for about 6 months which delayed building their clubhouse. Anthony Albanese a member of the Rudd Government would later give the go ahead for these funds to be reinstated. The project was too far down the track by then to stop, but it did look shaky for a while. In 2015 during a by election the federal government committed another million dollars to extensions at Port Bouvard Surf Life Saving Club.

During 2009 local council elections were held in Mandurah and candidates were eager to promote their success around town. The mayor was up for re-election and her advertising for re-election in the local press contained prominent information about the success of the Port Bouvard Surf Life Saving Club facility. Some of our members were a little uneasy and others commented about this style of advertising that in a way put one club in the spotlight ahead of the other. The Mayor's ward was Dawesville, the suburb in which Port Bouvard Surf Life Saving Club is located, and she was re elected as she was a popular hard working leader with commitment to Mandurah.

Coastal Times 23 September 2009

Worried About The Future

Mandurah Mail 24 September 2009

Chapter 7

Surf Life Saving

Surf life saving is the core reason for existence of a surf life saving club. Life saver retention without facilities is difficult and it was largely the same people in these life saving roles at Mandurah for many years. In the early days we existed with only one trainer, my wife Georgina for many years and before her Drew Bathgate was our sole trainer. Tony Snelling who later became the CEO of Northern Territory Surf Life Saving and his wife Julie both originally from Bunbury SLSC assisted greatly with life saver training in the early years for the club. The club lost members we trained to other established clubs or members just gave it away after a season or two due to the lack of facilities. Our surf life savers traditionally conduct a relatively low number of rescues and first aid treatments annually, however they performed a greater number of preventative actions. Preventions are the best form of keeping beaches safer and may comprise just talking to the public about risks on the beach or removing unsafe objects from the beach. I recall a few rescues and first aid treatments over the years and remember rescuing a child a long way off shore who was in trouble and not staying afloat at a council beach event in 2005. We had attended the event at the late request (in the week leading up to the event) by council as a few thousand people were expected on the beach and no water safety had been arranged. I hesitate to think what may have happened had we not been there or been vigilant. Our recorded beach patrol statistics are below for the period 2007 to 2014. These do not include statistics from water safety at special events away from our beach.

Year	Patrolled hours	Rescues	First Aids	Preventions
2013/14	1252	5	17	166
2012/13	724	10	12	169
2011/12	574	67	13	136
2010/11	585	5	23	167
2009/10	273	0	7	108
2008/09	295	4	27	152
2007/08	165	9	22	134

Our club was awarded The Premier's Australia Day Active Citizen Award for a community group in January 2009. This was for "Fostering Australian Pride and Spirit through active citizenship and outstanding contribution to the community". A plaque is placed in the paving to commemorate the award at the Mandurah Performing Arts Centre.

The award was recognition and a testament to all the volunteer work our small group had been doing in Mandurah with limited resources. It did make us feel good, but the ultimate recognition for us was our long term goal of achieving a club home that still seemed out of reach.

The club was also a finalist in 2009 in the Peel Region Business Excellence Awards in the Community Business category. Georgina Webb, our only trainer for many years was awarded the Peel Sports Award in 2005 Service to Sport - Surf Life Saving and The Premier's

Australia Day Active Citizen Award in 2012 for a person over the age of 25 years.

Club life savers April 2010

Our Sunday morning patrols established a flagged swimming area at San Remo Beach for many years, while our inflatable rescue boat (IRB) patrolled to Halls Head and Madora and the vehicle to Town Beach and Madora on an ad hoc basis. A Council Business Plan 2009-2011 stated "Strategy 3.2 Improve safety and security within Mandurah"......"Develop a patrol agreement with Mandurah Surf Lifesaving Club to cover Town Beach to Madora Beach." Our vehicle passed around five rock groynes along the beach and at a groyne near Henson Street, Silver Sands accessed a pathway and gate to navigate past the second groyne. The rock groyne at Wade Street, Silver Sands known as fourth groyne was passable on most occasions from 2005 until 2009. However, when the council conducted sand renourishing work at a cost of over $140,000 in 2009, they also rearranged some of the limestone boulders at the groyne and erected a fence which blocked our access. During 2005 to 2009 there were rare occasions when we could not pass through the area after a storm or strong winds had washed or blown the area out. I queried with the person responsible at council why a wire fence had been erected on the beach to block our access. He was unaware of what was in their business plan or our past activity on the beach and became difficult to work with. He suggested on one occasion that our problem was "trivial" and belittled our volunteer work. He would not listen to our preferred option for access past the groyne, nor would he take onboard the fact that we had passed through this area for years as he had not been with council for too long. He showed little interest when I tried to inform him of our past experience at this area. His option was for us to travel up a steep sand hill onto a pedestrian footpath for 200 metres, open a bollard then travel through a car park and finally open a gate to enter back onto the beach via a pedestrian walkway. We advised that his option was unsafe and that the sand dune would most likely blow out, making it unpassable. He would not listen and began advising that our option was also unsafe. I finally gave in and agreed with him, as he was an expert in coastal activities and would not listen to our suggestions. He had an earth moving machine conduct some work in the dunes for our access and within three weeks his dune route had blown out and was not passable.

We subsequently advised another council person via email that this had happened and that our beach patrol to Town Beach had therefore ceased. The email was passed on to the original council manager who had conducted the work and he swiftly sent me an email attacking me and stating that I should have telephoned him and not sent the email. I avoided this person from then on and informed others that I found him too difficult to deal with. We did request alternate routes and they never eventuated, so these beach patrols to Town Beach ceased for many years.

When our club house was completed in 2013 we commenced our mobile patrols back to Town beach when access was available. Council had made an attempt by then to improve access. In early 2015 a council ranger queried why we were patrolling down as far as Town Beach? We advised that this was something council had requested and the ranger replied that he was not aware of that. Town Beach is a popular beach with growing attendance. There can be a dangerous mix of recreation bathers, swimmers, jet skis, boats and board riders creating risks which will compound as the town grows.

Fourth groyne is a small beach with a good surf break created by the groyne. It is popular with local surfers and is a great area for young people to learn to surf. The coast is fragile and council spend large sums of money regularly attempting to repair the area with sand renourishment. Repairs are carried out by transporting sand to the location at great cost, only to have the ocean move it again in a short period of time. I had surfed at this location for years and was familiar with the ocean and wave action. Rips can develop at this location and surfers on occasions are thrust onto rocks at the front of the groyne when they attempt to catch waves too close to the surf break created by the groyne. Our club has conducted rescues at this area since 1998. Fourth Groyne is shown below.

Fourth Groyne

I did also request a meeting with the same council person to discuss better ways of handling erosion and improving the area for people to learn to surf. He would not listen to practical suggestions and informed me that he was well aware of these aspects of coastal management so my input was not required. The groyne is curved and on a slight angle to the wave direction, which creates a wave swirl or wash out action in large swell. This wash out does not allow back wash to break incoming waves and so erosion is a consequence. When I suggested a limestone sea wall in an area he said that it would not work, yet there are five council installed limestone groynes along our beach to reduce erosion. A limestone sea wall to reduce erosion was also a condition of approval for building our clubhouse in the sand dunes, to protect the facility in large storms.

When our club house dream seemed to be escaping us around 2009 among other difficulties we told council that we would not patrol the beach every Sunday as we had done for many years, rather that we would patrol two Sundays then have one off until they provided us with certainty about when they would progress our building, and that we would only commence patrolling every week when we were given the key to the building. There was no reaction from them and no objection, however they did ask us to reinstate patrols every week and expand our patrols in 2012 before the building was complete. We declined, stating that it would be done when the building was complete in line with our original understanding.

During winter 2012 after construction of our facility had commenced council requested our involvement in providing water safety for an international triathlon event for over 1000 competitors in Mandurah that they were supporting in October. The weekend for the event coincided with the commencement of the surf life saving season. We did not have winter club training or events as we did not have facilities and it would be difficult to have enough life savers fit let alone even have an understanding who would be back for the new season with capabilities to perform water safety for a large event. I sent a request to council asking if they would allow our young life savers one training swim per week in the council owned recreation centre pool for two months leading up to the event so that I could have fit life savers for the event. This proposed weekly swim would also allow me to engage our surf life savers, many being young members so that I had an idea of capabilities for the day. Council were not receptive and they suggested that we should apply for a grant for swim fees in their pool. We asked them to apply for the grant on our behalf and the best they came up with was one swim a month for two months. I moved on from the council and engaged our surf life savers in other ways and had success although a little more time consuming. Our new club president Kevin Elms who assumed the role in 2012 managed the day well with triathlon organisers. I coordinated 25 of our surf life savers, with help from an additional 35 surf life savers from three other clubs. We undertook water safety without an incident. Kevin Elms spent many, many hours running between the council, event organisers and SLSWA to set up water safety for the event as one of his first tasks for the season in his role as new club president. It was an eye opener and probably resulted in a little burnout early on in the season for him.

Council then lined up another four smaller events for us to provide water safety. I participated in one more council event in which our role was unclear and water safety was not really necessary, then I suggested to others in the club that we should concentrate on our core business on the beach. However I was happy for them to be involved in the council events if they wished to, but no members stepped forward to help.

An example of other activities that our volunteer life savers performed for the community is tabled below.

Business/School/Other	Service Required	Event/Reason
City of Mandurah	Water Safety	Public Beach Party, Halls Head
Peel Health Campus	Water Safety	Annual Mandurah Island Challenge Swim
City of Mandurah	Annual Beach Cleanup	Annual Beach Cleanup during summer
Ocean Paddlers/SLS	Water Safety	Ocean surf ski races
RAFFA Retirement Village	Guest Speaker	Surf life saving talk to offer seniors opportunity to Act, Belong & Commit – Inclusion Program
City of Mandurah	Water Safety, First Aid & equipment usage	"Surfing Together" event designed for people with disabilities to enjoy the beach
Mandurah Senior Campus Ed Dep	Water Safety, Board Skills Training & First Aid	School program teaching children Surf Awareness & Safety
Frederick Irwin College	Water Safety & First Aid Officer	130 Students at Beach Carnival

Assumption Catholic Primary School	Water Safety, First Aid & Equipment	End of Year annual Beach Carnivals
Mandurah Baptist College	Talk and demonstration about resuscitation and defibrillation	Student awareness
Rollercoaster Music Carnival	Water Safety and First Aid	Water Safety and First Aid for public
Adventure Zone Youth Vacation Care	Water Safety, First Aid & Equipment	Water based Activity Day for 40 children
Mandurah High School	Community Surf Rescue Certificate	Running recognized surf science class that was part of curriculum
City of Mandurah	Water Safety, First Aid & equipment usage	Children's holiday program at the beach to promote physical activity & water safety
Career Enterprise Centre, Narrogin Ag, Mandurah Primary Schools	Community Surf Rescue Certificate Requalification's	Assessing Teachers in re-qualification for their Surf Rescue Certificate - Education Department Requirement
Peel Health Campus Cambria Island Challenge	Water Safety for swim event	Provide water safety for 200 competitors
Education Department	Community Surf Rescue Certificate Course	Training Education Department Sports Teachers in their Surf Rescue Certificate
DSR Peel	Junior Sport Development Day	Opportunities for teachers to gain new ideas & skills on delivering sport through physical education making lessons interesting & inviting
Local & National Triathlons	Water Safety & first aid	Triathlons

Every year a surf life saving club is required to enter into a "Life Saving Service Contract" that specifies what days and times the club will patrol the beach and what services and equipment will be provided during those times. This is a contract between three parties: the club, Surf Life Saving WA and the council. The contract sets a minimum expectation and clubs are able to undertake extra patrols if they wish. There is also a section in the contract that specifies what parties will do for each other, i.e. what SLSWA will do for the club and how the club will conduct its self. I had included a section in the contract for many years that SLSWA would assist us as required for club and facility development. This was never questioned and I don't recall a visit from any club development person to see what assistance we needed in this area.

August was a time of year when there were no activities at our club prior to building clubrooms due to the lack of facilities. Each year we would blindly fill in the service contract for the coming season while not understanding our capabilities as the membership season had not commenced. If the Life Saving Service Contract was not provided to SLSWA on time by the end of August then the club may be penalised by losing administration or efficiency points and this would potentially cost our club extra dollars from SLSWA for affiliation fees at the end of the season. Clubs that gain high administration points pay no affiliation fees and as your administration points decrease so you then pay higher affiliation fees.

Our club has an annual award for most patrolled hours that is calculated from our beach patrol log. I had received this award nine years running from 2005 to 2014, one year jointly with Georgina my wife, and, another year jointly with my son Jake. In 2014 my daughter Teá also won a new award for most patrolled hours by a life saver under the age of 17 years. Spending many hours on the beach coupled with being president of the club and the driving force behind our clubhouse development was onerous. In later years I would get nervous when filling out the life saving service contract as it was difficult to gauge who would be around to help in the coming season. Would I be on the beach for many hours again, and how much help would be available? There was pressure on us to follow the contract once agreed and we did take our responsibilities seriously.

During 2008 SLSWA introduced a helicopter for aerial surveillance of Perth and surrounding beaches. The helicopter flew down the coast to Port Bouvard south of Perth. I lived on the beach and often saw the helicopter fly past and then 10 or 15 minutes later fly back to Perth, each time observing that it was flying the same path. If the helicopter flew down on one path and then back at a different altitude on another path it might get a different perspective and better coverage. I thought about this for a month or two then sent an email to a few people at SLSWA with my suggestion. The reply was thank you however we do not need your input. The following season the helicopter began intermittently doing what had been suggested.

The following two pages are photos of our junior surf life savers and nippers competing in competitions and training between 2006 and 2011:

Carnival at Secret Harbour December 2008

Nippers: Adonia Barrie, Courtney Kemp and Natasha Reicheld at an interclub competition 2006

Surf Life Saving

State championships 2006

Club nippers at a carnival with Port Bouvard nippers in 2008

Surf Life Saving

Local area and intra carnivals during 2009

Nippers and life savers February 2010

Bronze medallion training for Peel Region Clubs held in my backyard in 2011

Chapter 8

Dream Becomes Reality

Our surf life saving club had received three grants for our building with the last being in December 2010, for a total amount of $1,810,500. Council was still non committal on how much it would contribute and when its commitment would be forthcoming. We had raised a decent portion of funding and our council had not been successful obtaining grants for the project. However they would be successful in the future with a State Government Royalties for Regions Grant of $865,000 and they would only need to contribute around $785,000 of their own funds generated from rate payers towards a project cost of $3.46 million for a facility that they would own as an asset on their register. The cost estimate for building works was $2.259 million with foreshore protection works, car parking, landscaping, loose furniture, professional fees and contingency making up the balance.

When funding appeared difficult for council we explored options of the club assisting with building or project managing the building in an endeavour to cut out red tape and reduce costs.

We had well qualified people who could have managed these tasks within the club including professionals from other councils. Mandurah council would not entertain this suggestion or relinquish any control.

At a meeting on 16 June 2009 council approved progression of the design of the proposed Mandurah Surf Life Saving Club facility with subsequent reports to confirm facility designs, cost estimates, final funding strategies and contributions. Council minutes on 24 August 2010 show approval was sought to proceed to tender for the design of the facility and it was noted that council had approached federal government seeking funding contributions towards the facility cost. In the case of Port Bouvard Surf Life Saving Club council not only sought funding from the federal government they had a team including the Mayor lobby them in person in Canberra. On the 28th September 2010 council approved an unbudgeted amount of $200,000 for engagement of architectural services and the preparation of designs for the Mandurah Surf Life Saving Club facility.

A 42 page request for tender document for consultants was subsequently advertised with a closing date of 2pm Thursday 10 February 2011. This document had a further 5 pages of general conditions for engagement and a 4 page sustainable design checklist. The design was subsequently awarded to Site Architect Studio from Perth and a purchase order for the sum of $135,344 for their services was raised by council on 15 August 2011.

Ian Daniels our Vice President and I had numerous meetings with Site Architect Studio, their consultants and council staff during the second half of 2011. During these meetings we developed our building design from the original master plan. The building plans were finalised later in 2011 and planning approval was granted by council for the building. The building plan is depicted below.

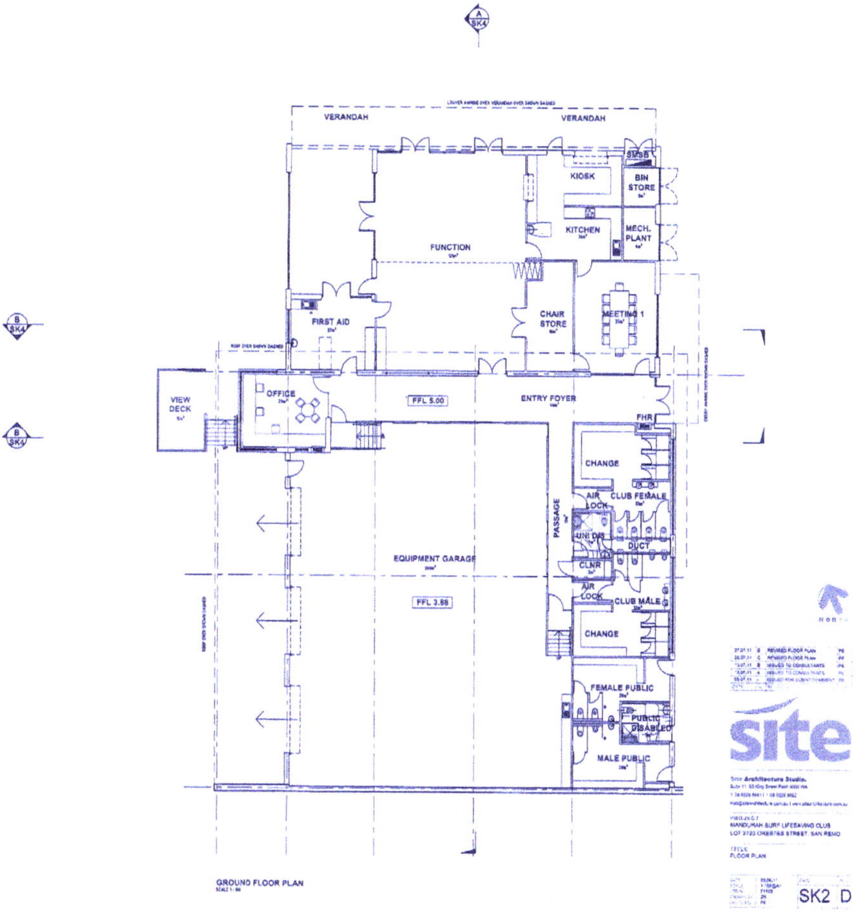

Dream Becomes Reality

Club Plan

Planning approval granted for local surf lifesaving club

Future design: An artist's impression of how the new Mandurah Surf Life Saving Club will look when completed.

PLANNING approval has been granted for a modern $3.4million facility for the Mandurah Surf Life Saving Club at San Remo, replacing the tin shed-like home the club has used for the past few years.

The building and seawall tender will be awarded this month with construction likely to start in March and an expected completion date in early 2013.

The new facility will include more storage space for boats and equipment, an office, first aid area, kiosk kitchen, change rooms, external public toilets, beach showers, viewing platform and a 50-bay car park.

Funding has come from Lotterywest, the Department of Sport and Recreation, Peel Development Commission (through Royalties for Regions) and City of Mandurah.

"This clubhouse is 10 years in the making and we can't wait to get it started," Mandurah Surf Life Saving Club president Warwick Webb said.

Mandurah mayor Paddi Creevey said she was pleased the first steps had been taken to create something that will benefit so many people in the future.

"It will meet the short-term and long-term needs of the local community and ever-growing Peel region, supporting essential emergency and first aid services for Mandurah's beaches while helping with training people in water safety and lifesaving," Cr Creevey said.

"Community facilities such as this offer a wide range of uses for healthy lifestyles, including sporting and social recreation, training, events, youth development, entertainment and fitness.

"As club membership, resources and presence on the beach increases, so does the need for better facilities and the new facility will help to meet that demand."

The club was originally formed in 1996 as the Peel Surf Life Saving Club at Halls Head and was renamed the Mandurah Surf Life Saving Club in 2000 before relocating to San Remo in 2003.

"Community facilities such as this offer a wide range of uses ..."

Mandurah Mail 5 January 2012

In early 2011 we had to seek an extension on acquittal dates for our first grant of $450,000 from Lotterywest as council were not following timelines that they had originally provided to these funding bodies during our grant application process. Lotterywest extended the acquittal date to April 2012 and expressed disappointment at delays for the project. They advised us behind the scenes that there were many good projects ready to go in the state that required funding and that they would have to transfer our funds across to one of these projects if we did not commence construction. This was understood however we were at the mercy of our council as it was a project that they had control of, so we in turn applied pressure on the council. I informed the council that they would not be happy with my actions if they allowed this project to be lost after many years of work.

Issues with the Council

During late 2011 council commenced a project funding summary for building our clubrooms. The summary showed their contribution as $1,650,000 and $0 from our club. This was circulated through a number of meetings to our dismay, as we had spent years of work and many volunteer hours of grant preparation to gain three grants for the amount of $1,810,000. We did manage after sometime to have this summary amended and the $1,810,000 sum was registered as our contribution. I had also commenced a building fund for the club during 2005 that would raise over $80,000 contribution towards fitting the facility out and purchasing club equipment when building was complete. There were many willing local sponsors and businesses that were supportive. Philanthropy is a great thing and shows a healthy community spirit.

It has been mentioned that council suggested years earlier that both Mandurah surf life saving clubs would be treated equally.

When they had entered into a lease with Port Bouvard Surf Life Saving Club for their facility a few years earlier, I had asked if our lease would be the same and they had reaffirmed that it would. I requested a copy of the lease and held onto it. Late in 2011 council began requesting that we commence lease and heads of agreement negotiations. I pointed out that the lease was agreed, however they engaged new lawyers and brought us a different and more onerous commercial lease document in November 2011. The lease negotiation took seven drafts and many, many unnecessary volunteer hours from me and Ian Daniels our Vice President. Finally the parties agreed on a document on 21 May 2012. This unnecessary process of renegotiating the agreement on complex terms and in a fashion that would normally be done between two corporations rather than between a council and a volunteer group that was to provide a mutually beneficial existence burned me out and left me not wanting to continue as club president once more.

Council was unable to provide lease drafts that allowed us to properly track their changes. I had requested this and was marking up our proposed changes so they could track them, however each time we had to review their full document again. Points of disagreement were over council imposing onerous terms on the club on insurance issues among other topics. I had engaged surf life saving insurers for comment and had surf life saving legal counsel assisting. Insurers had stated that if we signed the document that our insurance would be void and council were not listening. Basically council were endeavouring to take control in the event of a claim and were seeking the ability to settle anything without club involvement. Insurers were stating that indemnity insurance was between us and them and that we could not pass this right on to anyone else. It was simple to understand but council kept digging in and stating that they needed to protect themselves and would not listen when we said we also had a position to protect. As club president I could not sign such an unreasonable document, and to make things worse on 12th January 2012, before we had reached agreement, council asked me to sign a letter of intent stating the following "By undersigning where indicated, the Mandurah Surf Life Saving Club confirm that they have reviewed the Agreement to Lease and agree to enter into and be bound by the terms of the Agreement, in the event that Council resolves to proceed with the Agreement to Lease." It was another four months before we would reach agreement and it was totally unreasonable to request that I sign a letter stating we had agreed on a document before agreement was reached. I did feel like just giving in and signing things in frustration at one point, but that would not have been the correct procedure for the club.

I did request a meeting with council management in late January 2012 to discuss difficulties with lease negotiations. At this meeting a senior council person began telling me that I enjoyed coming to these meetings to criticise them. That certainly was not the case as I had plenty of more important things including my family and occupation that I had been neglecting. I pointed this out to him and he did settle down, however he said later that the project was only going ahead because council had supported the project by endorsing it. We had spent many hours since 1996 making their beaches safer whilst also developing the club and all he had done was endorse the project. I am not sure that too much work is required for endorsement. My dictionary describes "endorse" as follows "write on back of (document): sign name on back of (cheque, etc.); confirm support." The real work had been done since 1996 by club volunteers.

After the first year in the building council prepared our charges in accordance with the lease. They had given concessions to Port Bouvard in their first year but did not propose the same for us. We objected and they eventually reversed their decision.

Sea Wall Construction

A seawall under the dunes between the club building and the ocean was a requirement for approval to construct a building so close to the ocean. Our aim was to have the building as close to the water as possible to link the club directly to the ocean and beach and provide an appropriate atmosphere. There are a number of clubs in WA that are not able to view the ocean as they are set back from the shore behind dunes and their coastal atmosphere is impeded. Our neighbouring club, Secret Harbour is one of the clubs that did not have an ocean view before redevelopment in 2015. I did not want this for our club and we worked hard to get funds to allow for the seawall and a building within 100 metres of the water. The sea wall cost around $450,000 and it was paid for from our Lotterywest grant which allowed acquittal of the grant in April 2012 at the twelfth hour of the final deadline in accordance with their grant extension. Town Planning Legislation only permits development 200 metres from the coast and we had managed to reach a good compromise by raising the money for the seawall.

The seawall is 80 metres in length, the base is at sea level and the top is 4.7 metres high and it is covered by a sand dune. The wall is made from limestone rocks and rubble. The bedding layer of limestone rubble included 820 cubic metres of limestone and the wall is made of 3000 tonnes of 1 to 3 ton limestone boulders. Approximately 10,960 cubic metres of sand was removed and the project was completed in six weeks by a company known as Italia.

After the seawall was completed the sand dune was reinstated over the limestone. Building plans had shown a large sand dune over the seawall and we had requested reconstruction of a small dune but council would not budge on the size of the dune. This dune would mean that ocean views would be reduced from the club and we would need to challenge council over this.

Seawall under construction March 2012

Commencement of seawall works was an indication that the club was now finally being built after many years and this ignited some bad behaviour again with a few people that had previously objected to a surf life saving club being built at San Remo. I had been away one weekend and had left a life saving crew for patrol on Sunday. Access through the park to our storage shed was blocked that weekend as locks to the park entrance that provided our access to the shed had been tampered with. Our vehicle a Yamaha Rhino all terrain vehicle had accessed the beach via a pathway and driven from the beach to the shed and then towed equipment trailers back to the beach. The trailers were then returned at the end of the day via the same route and the vehicle returned via the pathway to its storage place at my home. We had registered the vehicle so it could drive down roads and council had provided us with authority to use pathways for beach and road access for operational purposes should the need arise.

A few days later I received a telephone call from a local fisherman known for his objection to our clubhouse construction who was complaining about the way our vehicle had driven down a footpath onto the beach over the weekend. I asked him a few questions and he told me that our large trailer was towed down the footpath and that vegetation had been damaged. I agreed to meet him at the beach after work to discuss the issue.

Before I went to the beach I spoke to the driver of our vehicle who stated that they did not tow the trailer down the footpath, rather only the vehicle was driven. He also stated that safety was considered and there were extra personnel in attendance to keep people off the footpath whilst the vehicle was travelling to and from the beach. I also measured the width of the trailer and it was too wide to pass down the footpath.

When I arrived at the beach at about 5pm I was met by two fishermen. One was drinking and we began discussing their concerns. The men were a little agitated when I pointed out that it was impossible for the trailer to pass down the footpath as it was too wide and that the vehicle was permitted to travel down the footpath for operational purposes. I asked where the vegetation had been damaged and walked towards the road with one of them and he could not show me any damage. When we got near the road we stopped and this person started a tirade of abuse towards me. He told me amongst other unpleasant things to f__k off back to South Africa where I belonged. South Africa was my place of birth but I had left the country thirty three years earlier and had lived the major portion of my life in Australia which I considered my home. It was difficult to stay in control with such abuse but I politely spoke back to this person for about ten minutes. His voice was very loud and could be heard a hundred metres away.

When I left the company of this fisherman a young person from a nearby builder's site had also joined in the attack on me. When I walked past the site he ran out yelling obscenities and chased me with an object. I ran home wishing to avoid this silly behaviour and reported the incident to the police. I later also called the owners of the building company who dismissed this person the following day. Some of the local residents who lived nearby spoke to me a few days later and said that they had heard the incident and commented that it must have been difficult for me to stay calm and polite as all they had heard was a barrage of verbal abuse being yelled at me by the fisherman, and they had not heard my voice. The fisherman's wife did tell me a few days later that I was the one who had abused her husband! All in all it was an ugly incident that left me a little bewildered.

The fisherman who abused me did telephone sometime later with an offer to help the club as he had seen a grant for security lighting for the facility. I quizzed him about the grant and in particular who was going to spend the time completing the necessary paperwork? We had actually explored this type of grant previously and our project did not match the criteria. I also explained this to him and suggested that he should direct his query to the council as they were the project managers. I did not want to talk to him after the past abuse from him and had to end the conversation.

Building Construction

Once the seawall was completed a builder, Smith Constructions, was given the go ahead in April 2012 to commence clubroom construction with a completion date of 14th January 2013 planned. It was two months after the start date before construction commenced, which meant that completion would also be delayed. Council staff were saying to me that construction had commenced before any work had started on the site, and I was telling them otherwise. Eventually the council called a meeting with the builder and there was talk in the council about sacking the builder due to their late start. We suggested that this would not be wise and eventually the builder commenced work with a plan to make up the two month delay.

4 SOUTHERN TELEGRAPH, Friday, March 23, 2012

New surf clubhouse under way

JESSICA PORTER

Mayor Paddi Creevey, Dr Kim Hames, David Templeman and Warwick Webb are keen to hit the beach when the new clubhouse is finished.

MANDURAH surf lifesavers are eagerly anticipating the completion of their new clubhouse with an official ground-breaking ceremony launching construction last Friday.

Mandurah Surf Life Saving Club members, Mandurah Mayor Paddi Creevey, Deputy Premier Dr Kim Hames and Mandurah MLA David Templeman officially marked the start of the $3.4 million project in San Remo.

The new clubhouse will replace a small tin shed the club has been using to store its equipment.

Club president Warwick Webb and his wife, Georgina, had lobbied the State Government and Mandurah City Council to fund the facility for the past decade.

Dr Hames said he remembered Mrs Webb badgering him about the funding.

"I used to play hockey with her and she was forever telling me off for funding the Port Bouvard Surf Lifesaving Club, so I've been pushing for this for a long period of time," he said.

"The council has been doing most of the work, their recreation staff and the club."

Mr Webb said the clubhouse, which will feature boat storage, an office, first aid room, kitchen kiosk, a community meeting space, change rooms, external public toilets, beach showers, viewing platform and carpark, would allow MSLSC to increase its membership.

"At the moment we've capped our numbers to about 200," Mr Webb said.

"When the club is built, you would think those numbers would double overnight and then we will have a lot more people in a lot more roles."

The new clubhouse will also allow the club to teach important surf lifesaving skills at the beach, instead of the Webb's backyard pool.

"We've estimated in the time I've been doing this I've probably put close to 3000 hours of my time into the club in nearly 10 years," he said.

The club is expected to move into its new home next March.

Southern Telegraph 23 March 2013
Site works commenced and then foundations and concrete floors were laid.

Dream Becomes Reality

The concrete was allowed to cure and then precast concrete wall panels were made onsite using the concrete slab as a working platform. Panels were also allowed to cure and then they were placed in position.

January 2013 Brooke Selsmark, Project Manager, Smith Construction

Club nearing completion March 2013

Car park work underway March 2013

Building commenced in earnest with teams of workers building and fitting out the facility. Towards the end of 2012 we could see that the completion date of 14th January 2013 would not be realistic but council were sticking to the date.

We had sold the club storage shed and I had been planning to finally move all the club equipment out of my house after many years of having it there and in my shed. I was looking forward to this date when I would have everything off my property but it seemed to be fading away with delays evident. Council offered another completion date of 8th February 2013, then March and finally we were handed the keys at the end of April before final completion so that we could start moving our equipment. Our season had ended before handover.

We had met with council staff that were project managing construction and the builder after the second completion date had been announced. Council staff were full of excuses which annoyed me and I walked out of the meeting in frustration and said that, this was the final meeting that I would attend with them regarding construction, and the project. One of the council staff members tried to call me back but I did not return and it was the last meeting that I attended with them. I left Ian Daniels and Kevin Elms our new president to deal with council on final issues and I continued with my life saving duties at the club as director of life saving and club captain. I just did not wish to attend any more frustrating meetings with council staff.

However, towards the end of construction I did request a meeting with an elected council member. I pointed out that the sand dune that they had reinstated without the club's blessing after the sea wall was constructed had reduced ocean visibility from the club. This created a false sense of security for people swimming in the waves directly in front of the club as surf life savers in the building could not see them. I also said that the club could therefore not be held responsible should anything happen in the blind spot. The councillor dealt with this simply and pragmatically and the dune was then reduced in size on the 20th May 2013 to the size we had initially requested, with views that we had envisaged. Having a surf life saving club that could not view the ocean would be similar to having a football club that could not view their playing field.

Brushwood that was laid on the reconstructed sand dune after the seawall was constructed in 2012. This wood was used by the public for beach fires, while people were even collecting firewood during the official opening. This brushwood was later removed and replaced with more suitable brushwood.

During the delayed building construction period from 14 January 2013 until building completion in late April 2013, council did provide two sea containers near the construction site for equipment storage. I moved most of the club equipment out of my shed, including a large 2 metre by 4.5 metre boardroom table that I had acquired with help of a colleague for the clubrooms.

The official opening of our facility was planned by council for 14th June 2013. Council informed us that the official opening was a ceremony to thank financial supporters for the project and the club would be given limited invitation numbers which was not ideal. Eventually we managed to have about thirty of our current and past committee people and some club sponsors included on the invitation list. All presidents of other surf life saving clubs in WA and Surf Life Saving WA Management were invited as we were told that this was protocol to invite them ahead of our club people/members. All local politicians, council staff involved directly or indirectly with the project, other government department staff and only five of the twelve Mandurah Councillors were on the list. I had requested that retired councillor Syd Wilson be included as he had helped me over the years. The CEO of Surf Life Saving WA accepted his invitation, however we were told on the day a few hours before the event that he had another commitment and would not attend.

Council sent out invitations without consulting with the club or considering acquittal terms and conditions contained in the grants from funding bodies. It was a requirement in these grants that the official opening was run by the Peel Development Commission and that invitations had certain inclusions. I received a stern phone call from management of the Peel Development Commission querying why we had sent the invitations out and not followed the required process. I was not even aware that invitations had gone out and was told to contact council and request that they follow grant acquittal guidelines which I did. Eventually it was sorted out and the Peel Development Commission and the council worked through their differences.

The official opening was at 12 pm on 14 June 2013 and it was attended by about 80 people. Various speeches were made including one by our club president Kevin Elms and one by Haley Hoving, a young surf life saver who spoke about her development at our club over the past three years including how it had given her confidence, new skills and the friends that she had made. The speeches from the Mayor of Mandurah and Peel Development Commission CEO thanked me for the decade of work that I had put towards development of our facility. The building was officially opened with a ribbon cutting ceremony which was then followed with light refreshments. That evening about 20 club members, mainly the committee and helpers returned to have a barbeque at the club.

Official opening, CEO of Peel Development commission Melissa Teede, Club President Kevin Elms and Mandurah Mayor Paddi Creevey.

Our building opening was not the same style of event as Port Bouvard SLSC opening that was arranged by council despite the promise of equal treatment. Their opening three years earlier was a larger event, with the Federal opposition leader in attendance, on a weekend with a marquee on the beach and it was more inclusive for their members with an event that carried on after formalities. We had tried to get a similar event from our council but they resisted and instead offered us financial assistance for an open day at the start of the following season. When we requested the assistance we were told we needed to go through a grant application process. This had not been explained when the offer was made. The assistance never eventuated as volunteers did not have surplus time to complete applications during a very busy first season in the building.

During development of building plans we had discussed with council areas within the building for club trophies, memorabilia, honour boards and sponsors boards. Despite these discussions the council lease did not make provisions for these items. We thought they were understood and normal practice as this had been discussed during design. However, after the first sponsors board was erected on a wall shortly after completion of the building we were informed that we had breached the lease. The local land developer, Madora Bay Partnership had approached us soon after our building was completed and offered us $50,000 to name a room for five years. This type of funding was needed to contribute to running costs, fit out, new equipment and new and unexpected costs. All councils are aware that clubs and not for profit organisations exist on such support. Using the word breach for this was surprising considering the background and the beach safety work that our volunteers undertook on council beaches without an operational contribution from council. Council had also been requesting additional club services leading up to construction of the building and they would continue to do so.

The first function in the club building was a dinner for a Rotary club on 15th May 2013. Rotary had helped us raise funds for our shed in 2007 and it was great to have them back again. A three course meal was provided with a club update and a talk from our young surf life saver, Haley. The evening went off well and Rotary donated a small sum to young club members. Shortly after this function the club had its end of season windup and awards evening in the building. This was a larger event with over 200 people and a few little teething problems emerged.

Our committee during the 2012/13 season struggled in some areas with a large workload leading up to building completion and the move into the building. We had seven committee members for nine positions and I held two roles as club captain and director of life saving and also set about getting new areas of management underway, such as facility and event management, building hire, kitchen and kiosk/cafe' management. Some of our committee members were ineffective at times, while there was a large work load which led to some frustration and concern. Finally at the end of the season we had new members interested in nominating others for committee roles. We had taken over nine months during the 2012/13 season to finalise a grant to equip our new facility with life saving and first aid equipment among other things.

Kitchen and kiosk/cafe' management is often a difficult and distracting thing for club committees with risks and financial burdens. Management requires business and industry experience and not all volunteers are equipped with these skills.

The incoming committee for the 2013/14 season brought a new president while two previous committee members rejoined with one new person. Still a total of seven with two vacancies and the dynamic and work coverage improved. The finance person resigned soon after commencement of the season leaving pressure on others. The club's honour board is shown below.

Mandurah Surf Life Saving Club Inc Honour Board

Year	President	Vice President	Admin Officer	Finance Officer	Club Captain	Life Saving	Marketing/ Sponsors	Education	Youth Development	Competition
2014/15	Elaine Daniels	Jake Webb	Rob Summers	Rachel Forward	Warwick Webb	Bob Swift	Vacant	Adam Hoes	Silje Harbun	Leanne Spiers
2013/14	Elaine Daniels	Georgina Webb	Vacant	Mercedes Barrie	Warwick Webb	Mercedes Barrie	Warwick Webb	Adam Hoes	Silje Harbun	vacant
2012/13	Kevin Elms	Ian Daniels	Michaela O'Loughlin	Kylie Hill	Warwick Webb	Warwick Webb	Susan Allan	Adam Hoes	Elaine Daniels	vacant
2011/12	Warwick Webb	Ian Daniels Kevin Elms	Elaine Daniels	Roseanne Polinelli	Warwick Webb Dane Stanley	Dane Stanley	Cameron Sturgess	Georgina Webb	Elaine Daniels	Georgina Webb
2010/11	Warwick Webb	Ian Daniels	Mercedes Barrie	Mercedes Barrie	Warwick Webb Dane Stanley	Dane Stanley	Cameron Sturgess	Georgina Webb	Mark Piercy	Georgina Webb
2009/10	Warwick Webb	Ian Daniels	Mercedes Barrie	Mercedes Barrie	Andrew Harrison	Andrew Harrison	Cameron Sturgess	Vacant	Narelle Frame	Georgina Webb
2008/09	Georgina Webb	Warwick Webb	Mercedes Barrie	Mercedes Barrie	Warwick Webb	Andrew Harrison	Carolyn Harbeck	Georgina Webb	Vacant	Georgina Webb
2007/08	Andrew Harrison	Warwick Webb	Mercedes Barrie	Mercedes Barrie	Gary Harbeck	Vacant	Carolyn Harbeck	Georgina Webb	Richard Bailey	Tony Bowman
2006/07	Warwick Webb	Georgina Webb Gary Harbeck	Mercedes Barrie	Mercedes Barrie	Kirk Bamford	Mike Gray	Vacant	Sue Gray	Laurie Harbeck	Marlene Renton
2005/06	Warwick Webb	Wally Fry Gary Harbeck	Mercedes Barrie	Mercedes Barrie	Mike Gray	Lou Carey	Georgina Webb	Sue Gray	Laurie Harbeck	Marlene Renton
2004/05	Wally Fry	Warwick Webb	Mercedes Barrie Georgina Webb	Mercedes Barrie Georgina Webb	Mike Gray	Vacant	Vacant	Vacant	Debbie Boekelman	Vacant
2003/04	Drew Bathgate	Wally Fry	Joane Fry	Joane Fry	Rick Fry				Debbie Boekelman	
2002/03	Recess from club activities									
1996/02	Thank you to all club members for their roles during this period, in particular the Inaugural President Drew Bathgate and his wife Maureen, later presidents Alan White and Bob Wintle and other committee members Mike and Claire Lathouras, Kevin Beard, Ross Shepherd, Brett Bettridge, Steve DeVries, Stan Bathgate, Glenn and Robyn Boddy, no other records were available.									
	Life Members	Warwick Webb								
		Georgina Webb								
		Mercedes Barrie								

The first season in the facility saw our membership more than double to over 400. It was a busy season! We had great support from local businesses which helped the club purchase new equipment for an increased membership. PEACH (personnel employed at Alcoa charity help) provided significant funds to equip our first aid room, mobile first aid equipment, purchase two rescue boat trailers and funding to manufacture a beach patrol trailer. This assistance was timely as there was a major first aid incident on the beach a few weeks after the first aid room had been equipped. A few months later there was another major first aid incident. The Rotary Clubs of Mandurah combined with us to hold the Mirvac Outdoor Summer Cinema in the Quarry Park, Meadow Springs which raised over $10,000 for our club. The event was arranged and managed by the Meadow Springs Developer, Mirvac. Channel Nine came onboard as a sponsor and other local businesses such as the Good Guys and local schools including Mandurah Baptist College, Meadow Springs Primary School and Assumption Catholic College held fundraising events to support the club. After these great steps forward there was a need for some recognition.

Surf Life Saving Western Australia has annual awards of excellence to recognise work undertaken by volunteers in the organisation. During commencement of construction of our building in 2012 the club nominated me for one of these volunteer awards. Our club had entered into discussion with staff at SLSWA and they advised that the volunteer of the year category was open for anyone including "people such as members who manned the club barbeque on weekends". SLSWA staff also suggested that after a decade of work that I was a great candidate for the award, however after an extensive submission from the club I did not even make it as a finalist. When I requested feedback I was told by one of SLSWA's employees that I had not contributed enough to Surf Life Saving WA during the year. This was one of the low points of the decade for me, hearing these words after I had spent so much time building one of the Western Australian Clubs for the Surf Life Saving organisation. A state body's existence is derived from the clubs that it represents and governs. I was never thanked by the Surf Life Saving WA for my work, however my club did thank me, and also granted me life membership. Georgina and Mercedes Barrie were also granted club life membership for their achievements of holding club committee and life saving roles for many years while running the club out of their homes and also being involved in gaining approvals, raising funds and developing our clubrooms. Club life memberships should only be offered for exceptional, successful service for lengthy periods and should not be granted too freely.

Some form of acknowledgment from our state body for years of service culminating in a very big year of service leading up to the awards would encourage and motivate others in our group. I am a person who speaks his mind and this often puts me on the outside. However it must be said that Surf Life Saving overall is a great organisation that fosters a healthy nurturing environment for youth and there are many dedicated members.

At the 2012 SLSWA Awards of Excellence, during the State President's opening address Coogee SLS Club was mentioned as they had commenced building their clubhouse at the same time as us, along with other WA clubs. However Mandurah did not get a mention which left us feeling empty. We later begged the master of ceremonies, Simon Beaumont, to include us in the evening which he did during a later address and this resulted in a cheer from our two tables of members. When the other club in Mandurah reached completion of its club rooms SLSWA awarded them the President's medal and various other awards including announcements in Surf Life Saving WA publications, yet our club the older one that pioneered surf life saving in Mandurah, was left out at the Awards of Excellence in the year of building completion. Surf Life Saving WA also incorrectly stated to some people, that Mandurah had snubbed them when disapproval was shown over our lack of inclusion at these events. Some club members were not happy with these actions and omissions from SLSWA, however club management had not made or endorsed any comments against SLSWA. SLSWA did not to seek any information from our club management regarding its position on these issues.

This lack of inclusion was evident in other areas, including the SLSWA, *My Beach News*, Edition Two – Summer 2013, that again mentioned the building of Coogee SLS Club and omitted any mention of Mandurah. One of our long standing members sent an email to SLSWA expressing her disgust about the omission as she was at the awards of excellence and also witnessed the first omission of our club. I could not help myself after the decade of effort I had put into developing a facility for club number 20 in WA for the surf life saving organisation, and I followed through with a second email to senior management outlining their short sightedness when it came to our development. I had also attached an email from 2007 highlighting their lack of support. We received a defensive response back from them. Later the State President of SLSWA made a visit to us and discussed this and other issues. We subsequently had an article in the My Beach News Edition Three – Winter 2013 about our clubrooms, after our official opening. Such articles should come about via an easier process from a state body that is working in partnership with one of its clubs, not through tension and lack of inclusion. Happily we received the President's medal at the SLSWA Awards of excellence in May 2014, but over a year after our facility was completed.

Chapter 9

Fathom That

Volunteering to a great cause for the benefit of the community can be rewarding. Dealing with local government and industry body bureaucrats who prolong and complicate things without always being open minded adds unnecessary volunteer hours which is not conducive to building long term relationships.

Australian communities function with great contribution from volunteers. There is sometimes reluctance from volunteers to step forward and help. I can now better appreciate this reluctance after my challenging experience. Regular turnover at short intervals on volunteer committees makes regulatory bodies such as councils and state bodies less accountable as background and information on their undertakings can fade or be lost when volunteers leave and their replacements enter an unfamiliar scene.

Statistics on councils around the country over the past century show that Western Australia has resisted change whilst other states have consolidated and reduced council numbers substantially. The table below shows council numbers in Australian States from 1910 to 2008. (Statistics from Graham Sansom, Dynamics of local

Government Reform, Australian Centre of Excellence for Local Government)

	1910	1991	2008
New South Wales	324	176	152
Victoria	206	210	79
Queensland	164	134	73
South Australia	175	122	71
Western Australia	147	138	142

A general apology was made to me and the club during an address at a council function that I attended in December 2013. A senior council person who made the apology walked over to me, shook my hand and reaffirmed his apology after the address. After ten years at the receiving end of a process that they controlled it was difficult to accept a short apology and forget what happened without being cynical.

Our local government system in WA has numerous chief executive officers (CEO) who are paid more than the state premier. Some back themselves into the CEO roles with lengthy contracts rather than normal employment terms. I recall a number of our local councillors responding to my concerns about council actions over the years by stating that local government is the lowest level of politics. If this is their justification then why are the heads of numerous local governments, the lowest political sector, paid more than the premier of the state?

Surf life saving discussions commenced in the 1990s in Mandurah initiated by the Peel Development Commission with contribution from the council shortly after. Our club began in 1996, with council suggesting that a strategic plan was required for the future of surf life saving in Mandurah. I am not aware that they developed a conclusive strategic plan and by late 2003 the town had two surf life saving clubs at either end of town, neither with facilities. In 2010 the junior club had a facility that was approved while the club had probationary status. In 2013 the older club had a facility, both developed by council. This was all done with the state body's blessing.

It became evident in late 2013 that Council Bylaws did not have provisions for a surf life saving club to properly operate on Mandurah beaches which suggested a lack of strategic planning or proper consideration during the development period since 1996. Council bylaws did not make provisions for operations of an inflatable rescue boat on beaches or in the first 200 metres of the water, or the ability for life savers to close a beach in an emergency, among other things. This was raised with council after the clubrooms were built and they set about amending their bylaws, a lengthy process. The management order granted to council for Eros Reserve among other things has a condition that includes "management of a surf life saving club" and these issues may fall under management or running of the club and oblige council involvement.

The clubroom building project was completed at the end of April 2013. It was understood by us that the surrounding park would be completed shortly after completion of the building. A plan was then developed by the council for redevelopment of the park, it was made public, and then the community was engaged for their input. Some local residents were upset that they were not consulted first, so their ideas could have been implemented in the concept plans, as the council seemed inflexible about adopting ideas and concerns once they had completed their plans. Nearby residents were concerned about a high, man-made sand dune that restricted the linkage of the park and the ocean and that large trees would obscure views. Parks in other areas of Mandurah had lawns, walkways or areas connecting to the beach yet this park redevelopment plan did not have great linkages or views of the beach.

Our new facility was initially in a barren area of sand and weeds with sand blowing around that often covered walkways. Sand entered the building for the first year of operation. Council had also stopped reticulating the park during summer 2013/14 and many residents were not happy with the lack of information on when park works would commence and why the park had been neglected without community consultation. The park was rough and almost impossible to walk on barefoot and five of the ten trees in the park had died. Small children living nearby were starting to use parks in other areas. Residents were contacting the council for answers and some were asking questions at council meetings.

Park works finally commenced in November 2014 and lawns were laid in December 2014. This work was welcomed and it did finally finish the area. Stage two of the park, incorporating barbeques and children's playgrounds was completed in 2016. Development of the park was largely the same as the original council concept plan and community consultation had not resulted in much change.

There was limited community consultation sponsored by the council on club operations in the new facility leading up to the club moving into the building. This resulted in some locals being misinformed on how the club would operate from the facility and a few complained unnecessarily. Public facilities and parks in a rapidly growing town attract people and complaining seemed illogical and could have been avoided or reduced with a community consultation program about this prior to the club opening. Completing the park soon after the facility was finished may have also resulted in less focus on the club, with focus also on new park facilities and thus more harmonious relations between residents, the council and the club. Project planning for the club started years earlier and planning should have allowed for proper completion of the whole area before moving away on to the next project.

Other local clubs have experienced difficulties when dealing with council over club development and their operations. Their committee people have frustrating stories of very opposing views and anomalies, with council often having the wrong impressions of volunteer organisations, their business experience and their ability to work and raise funds and pay off council debts or loans provided at construction time. Council own almost all club buildings thus make rules and agreements with other agencies that affect clubs and they often look for the line of least resistance for themselves and this is generally not the best option for success of the club. Working closely and easily with groups will foster harmonious relations into the future. There are many great people within Mandurah Council and issues raised are largely with council management, not councillors or staff.

There are also many great people in surf life saving. Port Bouvard Surf Life Saving Club's membership is largely new and amicable now . Most are not fully aware of the development and history of surf life saving in Mandurah.

Striking the required balance for the creation of liveable happy communities with facilities to engage and provide a sense of belonging to all walks of life, and building long term relationships and respect is difficult. I have learnt much along the way and thank all those who contributed to a great final outcome. Years of frustrating dealings similar to swimming against currents to reach this great outcome left me feeling like I had often been caught in a rip. Passion and persistence got me through.

Chapter 10

Conclusion

The final outcome is a great functional surf life saving facility for Mandurah with a club that has a sound foundation. The park, Eros Reserve, adjacent to the clubhouse has been redeveloped by the council finalising the project and leaving a showcase to be proud of. The club has evolved from a small group turning over a few thousand dollars annually to a strong organisation with a turnover around $300,000 per annum in 2014 and 2015. A healthy future is apparent with ongoing sound management. Club members will have a record of the club history through this book and the club should prosper into the future, embracing surf life savings many great values. Many people who frustrated our development and personally challenged me have now moved on.

View of the club premises from the road.

View of the club premises from the beach.

I have learned that change can bring out unreasonable behaviour in some who run wild on speculation without seeking out the facts. What is said whether correct or not is unfortunately often believed. People, politics, personalities and personal preferences carry too much weight in some decision making. Difficult decisions can make those involved in local government uncomfortable, and they will often seek ways to avoid tough decisions or slow decision making. During decision making it is evident that they are often so cautious about protecting themselves that they are unable to progress. Sometimes common sense may not prevail and this can impede relationships.

Conclusion

I have been criticised for things out of my control and on occasions for things I did not do during development of our club. My personal memories may enlighten others. I could not include every event that happened as some could not be written about. I agonised over all these inclusions and was asked to omit some which I did. Hopefully better ways can be developed in the future for similar projects.

www.ingramcontent.com/pod-product-compliance
Lightning Source LLC
Chambersburg PA
CBHW040329300426
44113CB00020B/2699